Gathering Sounds Too

Field Recording with the Rainbow Family

Tenali Hrenak

Muddy Boots

Cover Design by Jesus Velazquez
'Rainbowland' Map by Upik/Warehouse Work

Edited by The Venerable Ed It Tor
First Edition: 2023

Paperback ISBN: 979-8-9858987-4-3

Library of Congress Control Number: 2023914355

Published by Muddy Boots: www.gatheringsounds.org
Order Copies/Contact: gatheringsounds50@gmail.com

Also by Tenali Hrenak: Gathering Sounds: Field Recording with the Rainbow Family

For you...and all the trails yet to trod −_ −_ −_−_

Welcometh home,
Welcometh home again
It doth feel liketh coming home,
I heareth thy et'rnal song
Thee and I art one

AUTHOR'S NOTE

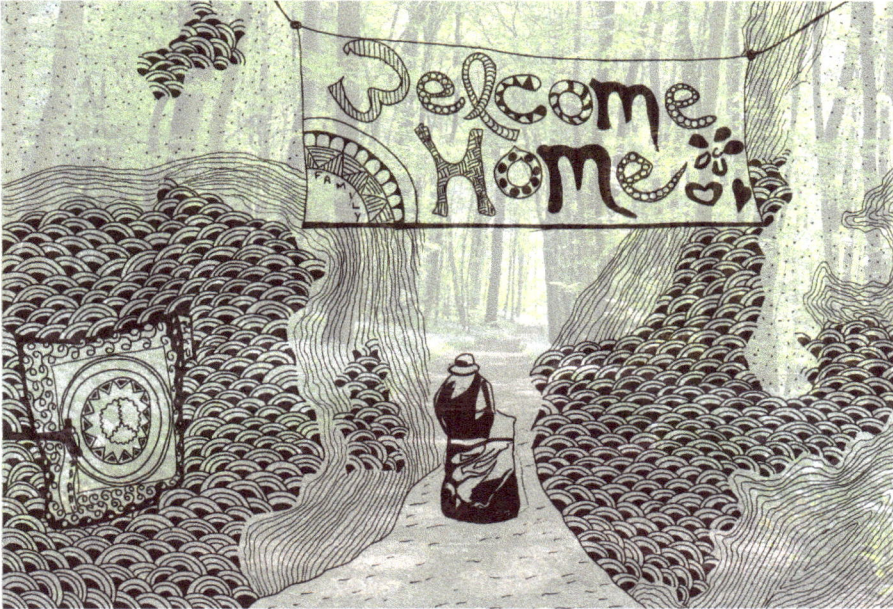

Art by Balthasahahaha Glendowertree

Gathering Sounds Too: Field Recording with the Rainbow Family continues sauntering through the audio archive project, *Sounds from the Rainbow*[1], featuring over 1600 freely available field recordings made over a 23-year period at Rainbow gatherings in the US and beyond. As part of this experience, you are invited to wander through 23 unique *Sound-Trails* (+ several meandering diversions), following a dreamscape format, which utilizes a *Rainbow Trail* theme to imaginatively walk within various gathering soundscapes.

We will step right into the *Sound-Trail* dreamscape adventure. For those who are unacquainted with Rainbow gatherings or the field recording project, I recommend reading *Gathering Sounds: Field Recording with the Rainbow Family* beforehand, as multiple chapters furnish a comprehensive summary and a descriptive account of the phenomenon/event, the factors that motivated me to undertake field recording at Rainbow, the various gear that I have used over the years, my recording methodologies (and snafus), and lastly, the primary camps and settings where I have carried out the recordings, in addition to musical genres and performers that I have encountered.

---

[1] Find the archive at: soundsfromtherainbow.org

Listening Note

To optimize your listening experience, all the recordings
mentioned and discussed in this book are available
to stream and/or download at →

gatheringsounds.org/too

The author recommends downloading the ZIP folder on the website
for offline accessibility and ensuring playability in case broken
links arise.

CONTENTS

PART ONE

A Sound Trail

Art by Round Robin

Alloweth the way of the heart
Alloweth the way of the heart
Alloweth the way of the heart shineth through
Loveth upon loveth upon loveth
All hearts art beating as one
Lighteth upon lighteth upon lighteth
Shineth as bright as the traveling lamp

0.23 YOUR GUIDE TO SOUND-TRAILS (TOO)

Art by Eye of Chorus

"Love is god, god is change, and change is love." —Rainbow Trail Soundbite

On a trail far, far away, a day in the life and a night in a dream meet at the crossroads of what songs, stories, and sounds may come....

Welcome to *Your Guide to Sound-Trails Too*, where sky, stream, earth, and imagination encounter a brief embrace and glimpse into a collection of field recordings immersed in a sonic dreamscape.

The following 23 *Sound-Trail* entries (although, let's be real, more than 23 entries are included) showcase a range of musical styles, genres, performers, instrumentation, stories, poetry, and soundscapes heard at a Rainbow gathering. The aim is to highlight notable, inimitable, beautiful, and eclectic performances, including everything from the amateur to the seasoned performer and from those who have been to one or few to many gatherings.

Some have since crossed the Rainbow Bridge, and these field recordings are among the only ones that exist of them.

As stated in the *Author's Note*, there are over 1600 recordings in the *Sounds from the Rainbow* archive. The batch of recordings explored in the previous book and those featured in this one still only scratch the surface. To be sure, performances, instruments, and recordist imperfections are ever-present. Nonetheless, there are gems and gems a-plenty worth exploring if you wander through the archive.

At the onset of each entry, you will find an accompanying photo or illustration. Interspersed within each *Sound-Trail* are various *Rainbow Trail Soundbites*[2], random trailside *Love is..*.[3]. examinations, and topical quotes from multiple sources. Many entries include song lyrics or story text to further illuminate the recording.

The *Sound-Trails* traverse through a menagerie of narrative flavors and poetic whimsy, prosaic and surreal, essayistic, folkloric, moony musings, autoethnographic, unique timestamp intrigues, and contemplative and performative writing styles. View these pastiches of interspersing inclusions, like a meandering trail itself, in the spirit of free-flowing creative expression and the imaginative and ephemeral dialogue one may hear at a Rainbow gathering.

In the spirit of the free and noncommercial nature of Rainbow, the recordings are affixed a Creative Commons Attribution-NonCommercial-ShareAlike 4.0 International (CC BY-NC-SA 4.0) license, and the recordings are intended to be freely shared and shared freely.

- At the onset of each *Sound-Trail* entry will be a prompt to listen to the recording— e-book readers, you are just a click away. If you read via the good old-fashioned hardcover or paperback, to listen to a recording, visit: gatheringsounds.org/too
- To 'click-to-play' an entry, scroll to find your selected recording. Press play, and *Voila!*
- Also, on said website, you will find a link to download the *Sound-Trails Too* (ZIP) folder, which features the recordings highlighted in this book. Downloading is recommended for listening offline if broken links surface, which happens. Then,

---

[2] While trail walking at a Rainbow gathering, many have remarked the unique conversational snippets they hear while they pass by others. These snippets run the gamut between profane to profound and everywhere in between.

[3] These were collected by Kristen Blinne at several Rainbow gatherings while sitting beside a trail asking passersby to finish the prompt: "Love is..."

unzip, and open in your preferred media player.

Of note: the 2004 *California*, the 2005 *Panama*, 2005 *Mexico*, 2005 *West Virginia*, and 2006 *Colorado* compilations, in the height of the DIY production and distribution method of the CD era, I spliced in various outtakes at the end of each track, following a gapless playback style. A friend, mentor, and fellow community radio broadcaster, the late great Mikhail Graham, once remarked how I do something similar on my radio show and podcast productions. He called these ephemeral bits the *tweeners*. Besides being a creative outlet, inserting outtakes allowed me to include aural elements that I found fascinating, but the time constraints of a compact disc limited what I could present. Now, when I hear these outtakes, they often jostle a fond memory and, hopefully, are also intriguing for others as well. A few of the *Sound-Trail* entries featured herein include these outtakes, and I'll elucidate further when we come across them.

You will discover decimal-point numbered diversions included throughout. These— mostly but not always—succinct entries and occasionally irreverent vignettes represent the *tweeners* between many of the *Sound-Trails*. If they have a decimal point, you have landed on one. Visit these as you see fit; turn the page following an entry and see what might be; sometimes, just by chance, and not too likely, you might discover what you (probably) were not looking for. At the very least, you will encounter an interesting recording. Anyway, if you ever find yourself lost, listen to the beat of the drums and follow that *Sound-Trail* back home. That, or simply flip the page one way or the other.

In short, *tweener* decimal point diversions and meanderings indicate the wiggly, surreal nature of dreams and the squiggly, nonlinear pathways of the *Rainbow Trail*.

The narrative that follows each entry comes gift-wrapped in a dream theme. Within this section, the boundary between fiction and nonfiction blurs, akin to the seesaw that oscillates between the waking world and dreams.

You and YOU alone are in charge of what *Sound-Trail* to pursue. You are the protagonist—the shining star in your own dream-movie. You are free to embark upon a trail of your own choosing, flip around the book and read selections randomly, follow the traditional cover-to-cover pathway, or scout the unconventional reverse route. This book offers a plethora of golden greats, timeless jewels, and delightful treasures, so whatever pace you choose to take, distinctiveness awaits.

The field recordings presented in this book have not been "staged" nor aurally enhanced post-production. Instead, the (quasi-found) sounds appear as is—raw and imperfect. By doing so, I believe, as Daniel Makagon and Mark Neumann write in their book, *Recording*

Culture: Audio Documentary and the Ethnographic Experience:

"To listen to the world as captured through a microphone and subsequently heard through headphones or stereo speakers is to grasp a sensory experience of a present. That is, recorded sounds—regardless of their temporality—preserve a sense of presence and immediacy that places the listener in a scene."

Thus, embark on a journey into this aural ethnographic narrative within an incredibly sound-rich environment—Rainbow gatherings—a phenomenon not often explored or showcased through such a medium. In keeping with this spirit, aural ethnographies have the capacity to do something that textual and visual ethnographies do not, insomuch that they offer listeners an opportunity to experience a cultural community as it is unfolding in the present moment and place of the recording as experienced within the interpretive environment of the listener's imagination.

Recordings allow us to visit the past, which, in turn, shows us the past is still here in the present, often informing us about the future to come. Life is indeed a stony, dreamy circle. May your dream-wandering and trail-weaving warm your heart, ease your mind, and soothe your soul.

By and by, there truly is no place like home.

So, without further askew, let's saunter ~ ~ ~ ~ ~ ~ ~ ~

0.42 MAP AS IT IS, IT IS A PAM

Art by Ski Matix

~ [|] ~

Eeny, meeny, miny, map
Catch a compass by the 'row
If it hollers let it show
Eeny, meeny, miny, map

0.66 ⅔ STITCH & WITCH – ROCK DOVE SONG

Art by Bog of Consequence

***** Sound-Trail Opening *****

Recorded at the 2023 New Hampshire Annual Rainbow Gathering, held in the White Mountain National Forest near the town of Berlin, and featured on the *New Hampshire 2023* compilation

LISTEN: ♫ <u>0.66 2/3 Stitch & Witch - Rock Dove Song</u> [2:37] ♫

Hark the rain doth drip and drop, hear the footsteps slog and schlop...
Now over the bridge and through the woods across the bog we go
The trail be muddy but the love surrounds as we move and flow
Hurrah for the meadow, hurrah for the fairy fire glow
May the land of inconsistent enchantment banish all woe

In consensual reality, we gathered near the Ammonoosuc River at the New Hampshire gathering. Ammonoosuc in Abnaki means "fish place" or "small, narrow fishing place." It is a verdant, lush forest; when the mosquitos (mostly) subsided, it was an inviting forest to camp in despite the rain. Memorable soundscapes I enjoyed include the babbling brooks (sometimes I heard whispering voices conversing in the flowing sounds), the evening birds (especially the one that sounded like a laser beam from a 1960s SciFi flick), and rain droplets (an idyllic sleep aid sound).

During seed camp, people spoke about the fantasy-like essence the site evoked. Various inventive names arose as a result. People nicknamed the site The Land of Inconsistent Enchantment. Inconsistent due to the weather and consistent rainfall. More names dished out an assortment of playful landmark identifiers, such as The Bog of Mild Inconvenience, Forbidden Zone of Electric Wizards, The Bog of Despair, Moose Heaven, The Bog of Regret, The Bridge to Know Where, The Brook of Watery Whispers, The Bog of Evermore, The Pond of Danger (inspired by the nearby Princess Bride-y named Pond of Safety), The Oracle of the Tiny Waterfall, and The Swamp of Sustained Wetness.

On the evening of July 3rd, Stitch & Witch camp hosted an Open Mic with assorted old-time music, round songs, and a cappella. It was lovely. One scrumptious tune followed another. It rained nearly the entire time, but the vibe remained kind.

Average Joey, the "Poet with a Banjo," did a marvelous job as MC, performer, and round song leader. About two dozen people huddled under a patchwork of tarps, a small fire was burning and laboriously kept aflame due to soggy wood (listen closely between [0:40-0:48] for fire troll poll blows). Comforting tea was also brewed and served. The rain ensured little movement scattered about to and fro, and people listened intently. Various performers played a song or few, and the night ended with them performing together.

Rock Dove Song, arranged and led by Average Joey, is done in a round style. A musical round is a composition where multiple voices sing the melody at either the unison or octave, with each voice commencing at distinct moments. The key is singing together rather than worrying about achieving perfect harmony. I like the subtle spooky sounds from the musical saw accompanying the singing.

   While recording, I wasn't sure how the persistent raindrops would sound blended with the music. From my listening point of view, it turned out alright—the charms of field recording in full display. The rain droplets are reminiscent of an old scratchy 78rpm shellac record. I hope the drippy sounds add vivid tonal color rather than distract or disrupt when you listen.

Sing me to the East,
Sing me to the west
Sing for me a melody, the one that you like the best
The rock dove wears the city
His wings adorned with thorns
The owl remembers the day you die as well as the hours you're born

   Something is happening in this universe consisting of non-simultaneously apprehended trails (*wink* Bucky Fuller *wink*), and we may never know what, yet marvel we surely must, in a dream musing strut, 'fore soon we return to dust...

1. RACCOON – NATURE'S CATHEDRAL

Art by Jamba 'Dives-Deep' Stuffworth

Recorded at the 2001 Idaho Annual Rainbow Gathering, held in the Boise National Forest near the town of Stanley, and featured on the *Idaho 2001* compilation

LISTEN:♫ 1. Raccoon – Nature's Cathedral [2:37] ♫

"Welcome Home Sibling Bear Verdant Forest Faerie Dirty Kid Punk"
—Rainbow Trail Soundbite

In *Gathering Sounds*, we explored the medley *Trippin'/Dumpster Diver* by songster and raconteur Raccoon. *Nature's Cathedral* was also recorded the same night at San Francisco Theater. Near the fire, a tie-dye tapestry hung between two conifers, marking the performance space where Raccoon sat on a downed log. Thus, despite the camp's moniker, the theater was a campfire rather than a constructed stage. However, simplicity more than sufficed; a campfire is quite theatrical, especially the more you stare into one. A few dozen of us huddled around, listening with enchantment and amusement. The campfire's flickering light revealed Raccoon's shimmering smile as he played his infectious folk tunes. He was an exceptional talent, a legendary street musician and songwriter. All the songs I recorded that night are quite stellar. The wanderlust-inspired lyrics made *Nature's Cathedral* a suitable selection to commence *Gathering Sounds Too*.

> *I'm heading back out to Nature's Cathedral*
> *To baptize myself in the river of life*
> *I set my soul free to soar with the eagles*
> *And I built me a campfire to light up the night*

Nature's Cathedral is a term used to describe the awe-inspiring beauty, magnificence, and transformative power of the natural world. It refers to the idea that nature can be viewed as a place of worship where individuals can experience a profound sense of reverence and spirituality. This song, for me, evokes the Transcendental movement that developed in the early part of the 19th century and the adherents' corresponding adoration for natural phenomena and divine experience.

> *And there's whisper and thunder in the sky that I'm under*
> *It cuts through my mind like sight for the blind*
> *The world that I want is too hard to look for*
> *When the world that I need is so easy to find*

The sense of awe and wonder from standing in a vast forest or staring up at a starry night sky can lead to a deeper understanding of our place in the world and a greater appreciation for the interconnectedness of all living things. In his book *Walden*, Henry David Thoreau wrote: "I went to the woods because I wished to live deliberately, to front only the essential facts of life, and see if I could not learn what it had to teach, and not, when I came to die, discover that I had not lived."

I lay myself down under blankets of sky
The flicker of the firelight will dance in my eye
I drift off to sleep like a babe in the woods
Praying my evils don't outweigh my goods

I like the imagery of the following verse, particularly the evocative simile in the second line:

I wake up to rain and I hear the wind race
The drops are like Pixies are kissing my face
It's so nice to be here and I feel so good
I will gladly trade iron and concrete for wood

Some view a gathering site as a cathedral or church, a place to connect, uplift, celebrate, and heal. The beauty and grandeur of nature can inspire a sense of wonder where individuals connect with the world around them in a deeper and more meaningful way. When coupled and revered musically—as exemplified in this lovely song—we can rest assured that the great outdoors often has the cure for all that ails us.

To the mountains to the valleys to the rivers and streams
With a pocket full of wishes and a head full of dreams
And I'm heading back out to nature's cathedral
To baptize myself in the river of life
I set my soul free to soar with the eagles
And I built me a campfire to light up the night

Audio Timestamp Indications of Memorable Soundings in Time:

[0:00-0:08] Inviting guitar opening lick coupled with nice campfire chatter: "Hear that everybody...last summer (?)"
[0:15-0:20] Background: "It's only like three generations old (?)" leads right into the opening verse: "I'm heading back out..."
[0:40-0:48] I like the interplay of the distant drum circle with the lyrical couplet: "And

there's whisper and thunder in the sky that I'm under. It cuts through my mind like sight for the blind"

[1:44-1:52] Impeccably timed finger mimicking raindrops follow the line: "The drops are like Pixies are kissing my face"

[1:58-2:00] A faraway yelp has a sweet cadence

[2:30-2:37] It kind of sounds as if the drum circle shifts into the foreground as the song concludes

Henry David Thoreau wrote one of his most famous lines in the essay "Walking," published in The Atlantic in June 1862, "In Wildness is the preservation of the World."

Before you have a chance to contemplate that further, although you'll undoubtedly carry the sentiment forward, Pied Pippie Pixie, who you recall—if you read Gathering Sounds, that is—gifted you a tarot deck made of gossamer, once again flutters towards you. This time, she waves a wand that leaves behind a trail of wildflowers that shower you like confetti. Swiftly, you're whisked away into a dreamscape where everything reminds you of our familiar world space, yet enhanced with a tinge of holographic shimmers that ripple through the elements. You will learn to adapt to this iridescent oddity.

She jests before flickering away as quickly as she had arrived, "Ye who roam the trail of imagination ought to be the one to choose what dreams may come."

An origami chatterbox made out of flower petals lands at your feet. You open and close it, and a poem written inside reveals itself. It coincides with your welcome embrace of springtime into summer and the dream-trip to come:

~ - ~ The Prancing Spring Stoker ~ - ~

Oh, what a bundle of jocund charm births
in beautiful boxes!
What insightful ooze springs
from sweet and simple things!
What anchored joy from chirping
tines connection coaxes,
Scrubs the painful, troubled goofs
For everyone, it's true!

Columbines, elegant shape of springs
happy extravaganza,
Her radiant wimples
Churns eyelids and dimples

When nature dines in flowered wine
Aged in the seasons turning,
She welcomes the waking
To share in the making—

Then anointed butterflies flap
like sly majestic fairies

Much amusement transpires
in flickering campfires;

And stringed oddities snare a glare
in unexpected prairies

Toes snuggle, rekindle,
Perfumed in earth fragrance.

A time possessed

of such rapture
Cannot regress
and be captured—

Great is the call
in valley deep
This echo drawl
a memory keep

If you commence in happenstance
—it's all you'll have to say
Like a baptized budding blossom
reveals a sunny day

A good spring trickles endlessly sprung,
Makes dresses lift like tickled hips—

And lips yearn for smackeroos,
Make jazz snaps of your blues

Then honey bees buzz like anything, when
a canvas evokes lush lathering fields

Popped cork and sappy juice
are not without their use.

No longing of before to stir
whose anxious spines we pay no mind—

Alive the dandelion,
In lustful eyes, they rise

Chuckling, too, what one can do with
a body let loose from a noose—

And drizzle succulent eyes
Dripping sensual divine!

Then snap tongue clasps
And frolicked bursts—
And oak song gasps
On rekindled thirsts—

And gooey slugs
on forest floors—
And watery jugs—
on gated doors

Painted supreme in ecstasy,
Amusing licks of spring
Upon her fair bloomy wild whips
Such delights come to DING!

2. DEJA, NAKILA, SASHA, NASTASSIA, TINA, & LUCIE – BUILDING A BRIDGE

Art by Bridgette Miak Begapode

Recorded at the 2004 California Annual Rainbow Gathering, held in the Modoc National Forest near the town of Likely, and featured on the *Leftovers 2000-2008* compilation

LISTEN:♫ 2. Deja, Nakila, Sasha, Nastassia, Tina, & Lucie – Building A Bridge [3:21] ♫

"Love is the way" —Rainbow Trail Soundbite

With each delicate thread spun, the spinner's hands move in a graceful dance, intertwining stories and aspirations. The spinner weaves an intricate braid, building bridges between hearts and minds, creating a web of unity that shimmers under the moonlight of shared purpose...

Gathering Sounds included a *Sound-Trail* entry, *Maha Mrityunjaya/Om Mama Le/Durga Stuti/Govinda Jaya Jaya,* transcendent and hypnotically sung mantras, by the same group of women that are featured on this chant, *Building A Bridge.* That night, they all shared songs and accompanied each other on vocals and/or various instruments, such as harmonium, guitar, djembe, and shekere. I recorded around a dozen songs at Jerusalem Camp that night, all fantastic. Following a wonderful Shabbat dinner at Jerusalem Camp, everyone was invited to gather around the fire for an evening of women's music.

Building a bridge of soul
Building a bridge of Rainbows
Building a bridge of soul
Across the land, across the land
We are building a bridge of soul

The concept of building bridges rather than walls is a metaphorical expression that suggests promoting connection and cooperation instead of division and separation. It is a call to overcome differences and work towards common goals and ultimately for the common good, rather than creating barriers that prevent communication and cooperation. What better way than through music:

We are building a bridge across the land
Music is the language we understand
We are building a bridge across the land
Music is the language we understand

While everyone slowly gathered around the fire, I arranged to record with a few of the performers I had previously met (and recorded). I found a good spot by the fire within

proximity to where the assorted performers sat. After a brief introduction, the music began. It has since become one of my all-time favorite recording sessions. Every song in the archive from that night is infectiously beautiful, timeless, and universal:

We got one love and one song
Universe won't you sing along
We got one love and one song
Universe won't you sing along

In addition to the vocal harmonies, we hear a djembe (or two) maintain a pulsating groove. A shekere shakes a rhythmic flicker that welcomes us to move our bodies.

You got to give it up to the spirit above
We are all made for love
You got to give it up to the spirit above
We are all made for love

Building bridges means promoting inclusivity and dialogue rather than resorting to aggression or dehumanizing others. It involves recognizing our interdependence and finding ways to work together to address common challenges. Increased understanding, cooperation, and collaboration can help to manage conflict and promote community engagement. By recognizing and respecting differences, seeking common ground, and working towards shared goals, we can build a more peaceful, equitable, and prosperous world for everyone.

Though Rainbow gatherings have flaws and missteps, to be sure, playing music together and sharing free food serve as a foundation for nurturing mutual aid and solidarity. This bridge of noble endeavor becomes a unifying force that brings people together, transcends boundaries, creates a sense of purpose, and fosters a sense of communal enrichment—cantilevers to guide you.

Building bridges is like being an enchantress of connections, using the ring of empathy and the wand of dialogue to span the chasms that divide us, unfolding a melody of understanding that echoes across the valleys of conflict. Bridges are not just material constructions but intricate pathways paved with compassion, inviting us to cross from the isles of difference to the mainland of harmony, where we may embrace the wonder of our collective human landscape.

The beauty of the *Building A Bridge* chant is its prowess to tear down the walls surrounding the most hardened of hearts. We are, after all, made for love:

Building a bridge of soul
Building a bridge of rainbows
Building a bridge of soul
Across the land, across the land
We are building a bridge of soul

Notable Audio Timestamps:

[0:00-0:10] Fade into a strolling rhythm
[0:18] The shekere enters the scene
[1:30-1:44] Nice swirling harmonies
[2:09-2:14] People yelp and hoot with exciting approval
[2:59-3:21) Shifts to a gentle, slow fade out

Everyone walks by and muses to anyone who'll listen: "As the ol' adage goes: Build a 418ft wall, and I'll provide a 420 ft ladder. Likewise, build a bridge, and I'll set the dinner table. If the negativity bias were inherent to human nature, it would be present across all cultures. However, it is a trait observed in societies that prioritize individualism, exploitation, social hierarchies, and separateness. Friends, family, and all, let's band together and build a world that prioritizes peace, love, and understanding."
You continue to drift along a lavender-flagged trail.

2.3 FREE RANGE PICKERS – SAINT ANNE'S REEL

Art by Twirla Twostep

***** *Sound-Trail Diversion 1.0* *****

Recorded at the 2006 Colorado Annual Rainbow Gathering, held in Routt National Forest near the town of Clark, and featured on the *Colorado 2006* compilation

LISTEN: ♫ 2.3 Free Range Pickers – Saint Anne's Reel [2:19] ♫

"My friend Hottentot Buttonquail donated a scoop of stoned soup into the Magic Fat Kids, which made it rain, and now wet socks block consensus. "
—Rainbow Trail Soundbite

A predinner impromptu jam arose at Musical Veggie Kitchen in early July. Free Range Pickers, a guitar and fiddle duo led by Chris and Julie, were also joined by Henry the Fiddler on—you guessed it—fiddle, Peggy on washtub bass, Emerald Otter on flute, and perhaps one or two others. They all started jamming, waiting for the customary 20 minutes to pass until dinner was ready to be served. It is essentially two minutes of ebullient bliss. The final sixteen seconds spliced in outtake is a call-and-response Balinese Monkey Chant-type thingmajig that Fantuzzi shepered at Granola Funk Theater.

Saint Anne's Reel is a traditional Irish reel that has become popular throughout the world, particularly in North America. It is known for its catchy and lively tempo and is often played at contra dances and traditional Irish music sessions. As is often the case in the folk tradition, the tune's origins are not well-documented. It was first recorded in 1927 by Willie Ringuette, a fiddler from Montreal, under the name *Quadrille du loup garou – 4ème partie*. It gained further popularity during the 1960s folk music revival and remains in many fiddlers' repertoire.

While cleaning their bowl at a dish station, Mighty Musing Moose turns and asks, "If Sibyl shares wisdom in a forest, but no one is around to hear it, do they still make the ecstatic sound of one hoof laughing?"

They pause and bid adieu, "See you back on the trail, Moonbeam Lunabright~~~~~~"

3. SHINE DELPHI – IF I COME BACK HOME

Art by Thrice Homemore

Recorded at the 2013 Montana Annual Rainbow Gathering, held in the Beaverhead National Forest near the town of Jackson, Montana, and featured on the *Montana 2013 Compilation*

LISTEN:♫ 3. Shine Delphi – If I Come Back Home [3:18] ♫

"Schlep by schlep, shtick by schtick" —Rainbow Trail Soundbite

If this was a parallel universe, Rainbow gathering directions might go something like this:

DIRECTIONS TO THE 2332 ANNUAL RAINBOW GATHERING in the beautiful Doohickey Mountain range along the Crawling Creek in the great state of Gaearth:

From the hamlet of Whatchamacallit, take Kangaroo Court Road 420 cartwheels, then TURN UPSIDE DOWN on Pot o' Beans Pass and go 6.9 meters, and examine the stack of Magic Orbs. Then, TURN RECURSIVELY the Vision Council Consensus onto 420 LEO Ticket Road and travel the 23 blown tires until you see a town meeting at Doohickey Hall. Soon, very soon, before you know it, mayhap, you will almost come to a very long, meandering tangent over Sticky Oatmeal Pass. Continue to ROLL (or not) the purple dank weed and IMAGINE the Main Trail near The Heart of Thingamabob. Alternatively, TURN INWARD when contemplation calls, and merely HOP, SKIP, and JUMP over the Buck Dancer's Moon when Moose tracks turn into a folk dance, for the mud people are like the dirt people who got wet. But if you get lost, just be honest about it and MAKE THREE TERRASECTS in Euclidean 4-space conch calls until the ouroboros cycles around again, where the circle is complete and unbroken. *Remember to drive slowly, because if you don't know where you're going, you'll never be late. WELCOME HOME!

I'm glad you arrived safely and in good spirits. Shine Delphi performed his tender and heartfelt lodestar song *Come Back Home* at the July 4th Variety Show at Granola Funk Theatre. It is a touching performance enhanced by the backup singing. Even the cricket refuses to be ignored and stridulates in the mix.
Shine explained the song's inspiration: "I was thinking about my grandpa when I wrote it. He was a huge lover of the ocean and sailing. He was in the Navy too. He passed when I was a teenager, and I remember feeling like I had just started to get to know him. He had been diagnosed with leukemia, and I felt like it finally let him put his guard down, allowing me to put mine down as well. The song is me thinking about my grandpa but somehow talking about myself. Standing on the sand wishing I could sail the world as he did and then at the same time wondering if I left this home and made it back, would the people I loved still be there for me? When I wrote it, wanting to travel and find new experiences while feeling homesick, I remember thinking I'd love a big crowd to sing the chorus with me. It was literally a dream I would have of me playing in front of a crowd

and everyone singing on the chorus. You got the recording of my dream coming true."
Here's to letting guards down and making life-affirming connections~

Standing out on the sand
Watching ships leave the shore
Where are they going
And where have they been
Well, I wonder more and more

Say I'm much too young now
One day I won't be
When that day comes
You know I'll be gone
To find the answers that I seek

Come back home
You will be there for me
Come back home
You will be there for me

It's been two years or more
Since I first left that sea
Now I wonder
If I should return
But I wonder patiently

On one hand, it seems right
The other hand, it seems wrong
Cut these hands off
And I would be lost
Without a way to play my song

Come back home
You will be there for me
Come back home
You will be there for me

Noteworthy Super Sonic Stamps In Time:

[0:00-0:15] Guitar opening, people get settled
[0:25-0:35] Cricket shant be denied
[1:05-1:23] People join in on the chorus
[1:24-1:25] "You too!"
[2:08-3:14] Great singing throughout
[3:17-3-18] Sweet alignment between the coda strum and "YEAH!!!" call

Be open to your dreams like kindness opens a door for a stranger, they say. Whoever they are. We may never know. They are as elusive as this sentence. Likewise, poetry is cunningly elusive, too.
Be that as it may, Meritorious Mouse & The Forest Floors String Band sing an almost silent poem-song in an assuredly odd time signature:

~ The Sound Silent Tale ~

Sound, what is it, but henceforth it goes again
Slithering, swooning, singing sacred songs sung
Moves through us, trickling like a brook, making us look
It washes away the stones of the most hardened minds
One may feel as if they belong, swaying to their favorite swoons
Ephemeral flutes pipe the forever tunes from many-a moons
Making shapes in shapeless cusps that are here until it's not
Breaking hearts in booming bombastic bassy juggernauts

Moving bones and melting blood washing away like the tide
Whispers and chants and all the rapid earthquakes it shakes
So goes the juggle of notes, tossing and turning as it flakes
When we go onwards ever onwards so the sound surrounds
Then all of a sudden, out of nowhere, threads silken harmony
Yes—verily—yes even sound knows from whence it came
Hush hush, not even a whimper, not even a flickered flame
You know the story - you surely know this familiar scale
That silence birthed sound upon a wispy, longing, quiet trail
Sound waves and trills,"Trickles trickle, so sings the spring."
Silence silently says, "Ripples and ripples see it through..."
Silence remains silent not because it has all the answers
But because it holds the sound when it dreams away in sleep

32

4. SARA – WHERE DO YOU THINK YOU WILL BE?

Art by Aleratha Moonnice

Recorded at the 2006 Colorado Annual Rainbow Gathering, held in the Routt National Forest near the town of Clark, and featured on the *Colorado 2006* compilation

LISTEN:♫ [4. Sara – Where Do You Think You Will Be?](#) [3:18] ♫

"Rumor has it that it's pizza night at the ovens all the way down, Starbright." —Rainbow Trail Soundbite

I am sitting on a mountain
I am casting shadows into the sky
I did not invite it but the sun has come
And is now playing tag with my feet

Sara sang *Where Do You Think You Will Be?*, a poem inspired by the 14th-century Persian poet and mystic Khwaja Shams-ud-Din Muhammad Hafez-e Shiraz, more widely known by his pen name Hafez (literal meaning "memorizer"), at the July 3rd Open Mic/ Spoken Word Night at Popcorner (MCed by Diamond Dave). Hafez is considered one of the greatest poets of the Persian language, and his poetry is known for its beauty, lyricism, and spiritual depth. He wrote primarily in the ghazal form, which consists of rhyming couplets and a refrain, using a word or phrase from the second line of the initial stanza, repeated in the second line of every subsequent stanza. His themes often revolved around love, spirituality, and the pursuit of wisdom. Many of his poems also infuse a deep sense of Sufi mysticism, emphasizing the importance of spiritual experience and intuition in understanding the divine.

I am whispering to clouds today,
'Watch out for my shoulders,'
For I wish no harm
To all my soft friends

Hafez's works have been widely translated and continue to be popular around the world. His poetry has inspired many artists and musicians, and his influence can be seen in the works of other Persian poets and the broader realm of world literature. That said, criticism remains surrounding Daniel Ladinsky, who was inspired by/interpreted Hafez into English, including this poem. Various others have translated and published more faithful editions. It is more accurate to describe Ladinsky's collection of Hafez as an extremely loose essence rather than a translation. It's like an inspired, mystical version of the telephone game.

I was so glad to hear
That every pillow in this world
Will become stuffed with

My soul and beard

Whether interpretive or more accurately translated versions, I love the ambiguity of Hafez's poetry. His poems point the way, but it is up to you to take the first step. When Sara sang this poem, I felt like we all at Popcorner were walking together through the vivid imagery of playing tag with the sun, cloud whispers, and beard-stuffed pillows. The whole camp vibe was quite alright that night. There was chai, popcorn, and lots of good cheer. One outstanding reading or performance followed another: From journal readings to cello solos to pretty unaccompanied sung poems such as this one. The warmth of Sara's charmingly sung recital style and the way her voice blends with the crackle from the campfire colors the recording with a sybilline essence that is fittingly redolent.

I am sitting on a mountain range
I am a precious body of water
Offered to the earth
From Light's own hands

Multifarious Markations of Aural Stamps-n-Time:

[0:00-0:10] We open with a snap, crackle, and pop into "I am sitting on a mountain."
[0:21] Snap!
[0:28-0:33] Crackle~
[0:36] "Pop!"
[0:40-0:42] Humorous distant laugh, probably from the chai and popcorn prep area
[1:06] "Woo-hoo!"
[1:50-2:15] Groovy campfire crackle and voice interplay
[2:25-2:37] Smooth fade away (I hear a ukulele strum, I think)
[2:38-3:18] Fades into me sitting in a meadow recording the surrounding ambient sounds, which include chattering children, marimba playing, and a distant drum circle

Sensible Squirrel pauses from digging a shitter and reminds anyone in the forest who'll listen, "Now that we offered our mind to puffy clouds, mountain peaks, and perspicacious poetry, consider carrying this eternal sagacity upon the mythical path evangelizing one of cleanup's top wish list requests: more duff."

They continue, "Have you ever read cleanup's riveting and absorbing six-word story? It's won a number of literary awards. It goes like this:

"For trails: more duff, less fluff."

4.2 JOHN - KORA DE LA NOCHE

Art by Try Ang Ulation

***** *Sound-Trail Diversion 2.0* *****

Recorded at the 2005 Mexico Rainbow Gathering, held in the Sierra de Los Tuxtlas near the town of Catemaco, and featured on the *Mexico 2005* compilation

LISTEN:♫ [4.2 John - Kora De La Noche](#) [3:23] ♫

"I was an amoeba before the moon was full." —Rainbow Trail Soundbite

A late-night recording around the campfire near the bakery ovens, only a few of us were hanging out, and a waning crescent moon[4] floated like the shiny dreams of youth. John played Kora while someone improvised a lush harmony vocal. I love these kinds of impromptu jams. The strong wind that blew through almost swept away the gentle, flowing soundwaves. It was a battle between two rival sonic vibrations. Between [2:25-3:15], the wind pulsations blast through the area, causing a shift in the stereo image. Sometimes, this gives me the sensation that the wind is emanating from the speakers. Fortuitously, the dulcet resonance of the vocals and kora triumphed as though this recording had been fated for audibility. And so it is~

Before you have a chance to turn the page to see where the trail leads next, two Shakespearean thespians with deep dark eyes named Guildenslittrench and Rosencompost stroll by singing in unison, Pachamama, a familiar song in antiquated tongue:

Pachamama, I'm coming home
To the lodging wh're I belongeth
Pachamama, I'm coming home,
To the lodging wh're I belongeth

I wanteth to beest free, so free
Liketh the dolphin in the flote
Liketh the floweth'rs and the bees
Liketh the birds in the trees
I wanteth to flyeth high, so high
Liketh an eagle in the sky

---

[4] The word "Mexico" originates from the Nahuatl language and translates to "belly button of the moon"

And at which hour mine own timeth hast cometh
I'm gonna did lie down and kicketh the bucket
And at which hour mine own timeth hast cometh
I'm gonna riseth up and flyeth

Pachamama, I'm coming home
To the lodging wh're I belongeth
Pachamama, I'm coming home,
To the lodging wh're I belongeth!

I wanteth to beest free, beest me
Beest the being yond I seeth
Not to riseth and not to falleth
Being one and loving all
Th're's nay high
Th're's nay base
Th're is nay lodging I shouldst wend
Just inside a dram star
Telling me, beest as thou art.
Just inside a dram star telling me—beest as thou art.

40

5. SHAMS - STEW SONG

Art by Dsoelarti

Recorded at Rough & Ready Kitchen at the 2017 Oregon Rainbow Gathering, held in the Malheur National Forest near the town of John Day, and featured on the *Oregon 2017* compilation

LISTEN:♫5. Shams - Stew Song [3:57] ♫

"Whatever you cooked up that brought you here can't be undone with what you've been stewing, so you best be stirrin' what you got. Life might be short, but a song infuses the umami and thus merges with the other side's stock pot" —Rainbow Trail Soundbite

Recorded late in the evening towards the end of June at the Story Glory tent. Shams and others stopped by and played some tunes. This session followed a night of brownie making, so we had plenty of sweet treats—namely, rose-flavored brownies—to please our taste buds along with our ears. In *Stew Song*, Shams performed alone on vocals and guitar. There was another memorable recording session at the same gathering with Shams a few days later at Rough & Ready kitchen while stir-fried rice was being made. You can hear sizzling wok sounds on a few of those tracks.

You'll start to stir the bubblin' pot

Sharing food has been an important cultural and social practice that has been around since the beginning of the human story. It is a way to connect with others, build relationships, and express care and hospitality. In many cultures, sharing food is viewed as a symbol of community and togetherness. At Rainbow, "free food in the woods" is a common expression. The sharing of food remains one of the gathering's virtuous activities.

Add a little oil and turn your heat down low

Shams also goes by the stage name Dumpster Joe. A mutual friend, Shaney, introduced us. We all have a shared interest in music from the 1920s and 30s and record collecting, and Shaney and Shams played together in a few musical projects, notably The Dunghill Rooster Strutters (great stuff, by the way). Shaney passed away in the fall of 2022. He was loved by many. The 2017 Oregon gathering was the last time we worked together in a Rainbow kitchen. We had been doing kitchens since the mid-1990s, continuously for over a decade. We also worked together preparing meals at disaster relief kitchens, homeless shelters, Food Not Bombs, and activist demonstrations. He remains my all-time favorite cook. Most importantly, underneath his gruff demeanor, he was very kind and caring, witty to no end, the king of off-the-cuff one-liners, incredibly humble and giving, and easily one of the funniest people I have ever known and will likely know. Shaney once self-proclaimed "Imma hillbilly Uncle Fester with squirrel meat caught in his teeth!" to our mutual friend Erin, and she jotted that quip down on a napkin.
 One of my favorite memories from that gathering was Shaney making homemade pretzels while assorted jams happened adjacent to the prep area, from old-time and blues to folk and swing jazz. Shaney encouraged a recording session with Shams as he recognized Sham's talent and my love of field recording as a good ingredient mix. *Stew Song* slowly cooks a

mighty fine stew and imbues stirring a pot with nifty fingerpicking.

The best stews all take time to unwind

Food is a common theme in folk music, and many traditional songs celebrate different types of cuisine or incorporate references to food. Sometimes these references are direct, such as the Appalachian folk song Cornbread and Butterbeans (written by Don Whitson and first recorded in 1947 by Johnny Tyler and The Riders of the Rio Grande in 1948), popularized by the Carolina Chocolate Drops in the 2000s, celebrates the simple pleasures of home cooking. Whereas, at other times, euphemism wears the cook's apron when serving up a food song, sort of like flustering the sultry upside cake. Bo Carter's *Banana In Your Fruit Basket* is a nectarous example of this lyrical style or position (if you know what I mean). *Stew Song* is a one-part song of unrequited love and one-part food prep.

With the right spices, the flavor can start

Few things are more unifying than the act of breaking bread together. Add some music to a stew, and goodness awaits. Music and food have a symbiotic relationship, feeling completely natural when paired. Often, food tastes especially delicious in the woods. Is it the remoteness that makes this so? Or is it the love put into the cooking? The communal aspect? All of the above, I reckon. At Story Glory, Shams flavored the archive with one of its tastiest food songs. The bonus for me is that I love to cook, and I love a good food song. My favorite moments at a Rainbow kitchen are when a bunch of people work together like elves preparing a meal while one or more people are playing some tunes (food is ready in 20 minutes!). It's a vibe and a damn good one. If you know, you know.

So I'm gonna get up and get me a bowl full of stew

Bracketed Audio Waves Exist In and Out of Time:

[0:00-0:03] Fade into a rare glimpse of me speaking on the mic: "Alright."
[0:04-1:09] Delicious instrumental opening
[2:15-2:47] I can feel the stew cooking
[2:58-3:00] Nice giggly utterance of the lyric
[3:54-3:56] Shams says concisely: "Food songs"
[3:57] Fade out into a bowl full of stew

Folk music is—kind of, sort of, always—alive and well, in wakefulness, dreams, and beyond. As labor organizer, storyteller, and folk singer Utah Phillips put it, "A folk song is any song you choose to sing yourself," You nod approvingly, observing that insightful observation. You hover along. You pass by Lovin' Tropes Kitchen, and you overhear your friend and cook Jazzbo Hamhock disappointedly grumble, "I say, this knife is as sharp as mashed potatoes." You snicker. Then, you're asked to help haul in some dry goods and produce that arrived at Main Supply. You and others take flight and float at a steady pace. You look up. Cumulous clouds form words that resemble song lyrics: .

~Twinkle Twinkle Wonder Still~

What happens when you're so lonesome, and you've already cried?
Does that negate the song, or does it still apply?
With the bell rung, they say one must seek within and decide

But who's to say if therein an answer does abide?
It's sort of like the way we try to bite our own teeth
So, mayhap the glory we solicit lies with the wreath

Twinkle twinkle, ever so far
How I wonder and wonder still
Up above the years you fly
Like a bygone era in the sky

What happens when love discovers a lost trail in our quest?
Will it dissipate through time or continue with zest?
With the nectar tasted, they say we must try as we might
But where in the heart do we grasp the flowers of sight?
It's like the way we clap with one hand when it takes two
So, mayhap the lantern we light is our only cue

Twinkle twinkle, ever so far
How I wonder and wonder still
Up above the years you fly
Like a bygone era in the sky

Twinkle twinkle, ever so far
How I wonder and wonder still
How I wonder and wonder still

46

5.55 HOSE THE CLAMP

Art by Aquarum Flowalis

~ O ~

Steel serpent grips tight
Whispering ripples do flow
Scent of petrichor

48

6. GFUNK COLLECTIVE - TEA TIME

Art by Harch Mare & Had Matter

Recorded at the 2009 New Mexico Annual Rainbow Gathering, held in the Santa Fe National Forest near the town of Cuba, and featured on the *New Mexico 2009* compilation

LISTEN: ♫ 6. Gfunk Collective – Tea Time [3:05] ♫

"Love is the slice that cuts through time" —Rainbow Trail Soundbite

Keep your space
It's yours for sure
Pack your bags
Get out the door
You're goin' to Rainbow now
Everyone
It's tea time forever

Tea Time was recorded at the Granola Funk Super Dance Party Prom Revolution Night on July 2nd at Granola Funk Theater. Several promotional parades in the days leading up to the event occurred on the trail to and at Dinner Circle. As it goes with Granola Funk parades, people hopped on and off the wandering hootenanny and mayhem brigade as they roved along the trail. It always got especially zany engaged in tomfoolery circling around the Dinner Circle wearing costumery, draped in garb like a velvet cape and a papier-mâché mask. Musically, this was the most successful dance party that Granola Funk hosted. Everything just came together, everywhere, all with spunk.

Many musicians arrived with a variety of instruments in tow, including but not limited to accordion, banjo, guitar, upright bass, fiddle, harp, mandolin, trombone, trumpet, saxophone, didgeridoo, clarinet, dundun, djembe, darbuka, cajon, drum kit, and harmonium.

In the classic novel *Alice's Adventures in Wonderland* by Lewis Carroll, the character of the Mad Hatter famously hosts a tea party for Alice and her companions. The tea party is known for its chaotic and nonsensical atmosphere, with the Mad Hatter and his guests engaging in bizarre and zany conversation. Mad Hatter's quarrel with Time started when the Queen of Hearts proclaimed—in her opinionated view—how he had murdered Time when he delivered a terrible musical performance. In short, Time is thusly stuck at six o'clock for him ever since. Egro, during the tea party, the Mad Hatter announces that it is always tea time in Wonderland and that there is never a specific time to stop for tea. He also argues with the March Hare over the proper way to serve tea and its drinking etiquette. The spirit of the song *Tea Time* evokes said story and embodies it, given the dreaminess and the sense of "It's always tea time at Rainbow," energy that binds the Rainbow phenomenon together to some degree. Moreover, often, weeks or months after a gathering, it feels as if the whole experience was a dream.

Aslan from Granola Funk took on the de facto musical director role, providing guidance and direction to the diverse group of musicians in the menagerie. Still, otherwise, this piece, *Tea Time* (and all the others recorded that night), was improvised, including the lyrics whipped up by vocalist Alex, sung through a megaphone. A steady groove led by percussion maestro Elan Rae opens with an invitation to a tea party. The horns flourish in a wavy drone, leading us into a trance when blended with the harmonium. While the Mad Hatter's speech might be riddled with nonsense—"Why is a raven like a dish station?"—this improvisation is not. The late great Charlotte played the harmonium, featured prominently on this track, helping guide us through Wonderland. At [1:58], when the harmonium moves to the forefront, magic unfolds, the bell is rung, and tea is served, forever.

We're not leaving here
No no no
We're not leaving
It's our space
We're outside
We're not leaving here
It's tea time forever

Notable Aural Patterns:

[0:00-0:12] Fade into a smooth groove jam
[0:23-0:24] "It's tea time forever"
[0:59-1:05] Nice drum fill leads right into a robust beat
[1:29-1:31] "Feeling it, brother?" ... To that, I ask, feeling what exactly?
[1:43-2:15] "Hear, it's coming...the harmonium is speaking... do you hear it?" .... Indeed, the harmonium speaks in the ways of magic
[2:49-3:05] Fade out into "We're not leaving here...It's Tea Time forever now"

Your friend Space Elf hypothesizes whether or not humans exist or if they are octopi pretending to be human. You have no rebuttal, but as dreams tend to have it, you suddenly find yourself making a cup of peppermint tea. You want to taste it, but before you can, your motor functions disengage, and you start to glide along a tentacled polka-dotted trail that loopity loops as if time is an unknobbly circle on an obstacle course churning in the wheels of s(t)imulation.

6.6 TREE & MOHAN - RISE

Art by Le Tigreenhorn Floustached Mowerpiercer

***** *Sound-Trail Diversion 3.0* *****

Recorded at the 2022 Colorado Annual Rainbow Gathering, held in the Medicine Bow-Routt National Forest near the town of Hayden, and featured on the *Colorado 2022* compilation

LISTEN:♫ 6.6 Tree & Mohan - Rise [3:10] ♫

"Paint me a pick axe, and we'll read a blue tarp on the way to the spring of eternal twine."
—Rainbow Trail Soundbite

Tree & Mohan performed *Rise* at the July 4th Variety Show at Granola Funk Theater. An enlivening and infectious song that reminds me of the type of folk-tinged chants you would hear throughout the 1990s at Rainbow—old school warmly represents ~

We are tending to the sacred fire of our hearts
We are tending to the sacred fire of our hearts

We are dancing around the flames of joy and peace
We are dancing around the flames of joy and peace

Singing and celebrating life in harmony
Singing and celebrating life in harmony

We are the way showers
The gatekeepers of truth
We are the way showers
The gatekeepers of truth

And even through the darkest of times, we will shine our light—Rainbow light
And even through the darkest of times, we will shine our light

Day by day, we will climb, we will rise—so high
Day by day, we will climb, we will rise

What a lovely, uplifting tune—well done! As unannounced as a woodpecker pecks in a tree above your tent at 6 am, an assembly of Tinies march by you singing a catchy tune entitled, Tinies

Love You, This They Know

We are Tinies, hear us roar
We live on the forest floor

We are Tinies, big and tall
If you need, we'll heed the call

We are Tinies, not ground scores
We hope to end all the wars

Yes, Tinies love you
Yes, Tinies love you
Yes, Tinies love you
The refrain tells you so

56

7. SUGRA - AGRICULTURE SONG

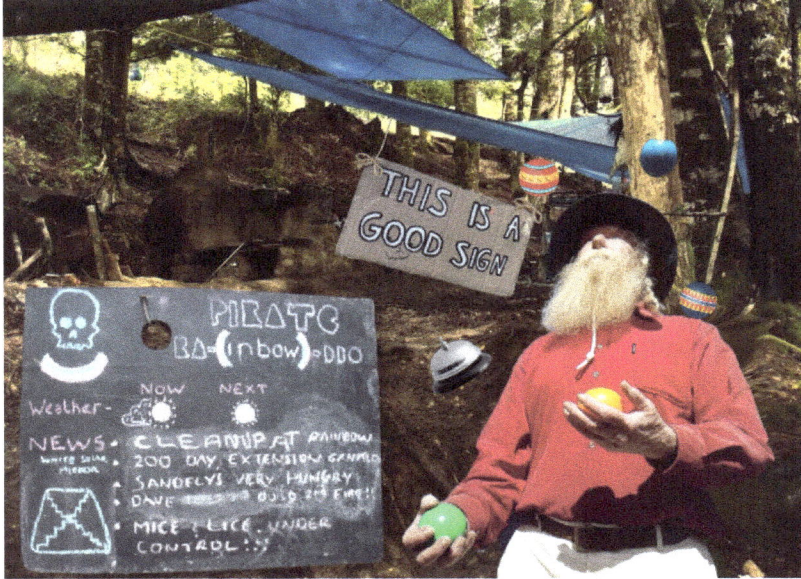

Art by Jugglin' Jericho

Recorded at the 2009/10 New Zealand World Rainbow Gathering held in the Tasman Region of the South Island near the town of Murchison and featured on the *New Zealand 2009/10* compilation

LISTEN:♫ 7. Sugra – Agriculture Song [1:25] ♫

"We croak so you don't have to." —*Frog Trail Soundbite*

Now there once was a farmer who sat on a rock

I recorded *Agriculture Song* at Whatever It Is, I'm Against It Bakery (sometimes also known as Whatever You Are Doing, It's All Wrong Bakery) towards the latter part of the gathering. Around a dozen of us sat around the oven, telling stories and reminiscing on the gathering soon ending. Juggler and storytelling extraordinaire Sugra charmed and tickled us with a few stories, jokes, and songs. You can tell by the giggles heard throughout the recording.

Shaking his whiskers and waving his fist at the people all gathering sticks
And teaching the children to play with their kites and their marbles and days of all yore

As the track begins, Sugra introduces it as *Agriculture Song*. However, in folk circles, it is commonly known as *There Once Was A Farmer,* a traditional song dating back to 1900 or possibly earlier. Although, as is often the case, the exact origins remain unknown. Sometimes, the unknown is all there is to know.

When along came a lady who looked like a decent young person with a face like a duck
They say she's discovered a new way to teach the young children to sew and knit

Oral tradition, by default, invites retellings, different versions, and interpretations. It's been told at youth summer camps to Ren Faires. Some versions are bawdy and risqué, while others are more tame tellings of cartoonish tales such as *Farmer vs. Rat.*

To poison the barnyard with shoveling mud from the stable and mowing the lawn
When along came the squire who pulled out his horse from the stable to go on a hunt

The melody of *Agriculture Song* is similar to the novelty song, *Shaving Cream.* These types of novelty songs are sometimes known as teasing songs or mind rhymes that date back centuries. Literary luminaires like Emily Dickinson and Shakespeare feature them in their works.

His wife's in the bedroom powdering her nose with some powder she keeps in a box
She's just getting over her last dose of gout and romantics, and it has left her all stiff

American singer and actress Dinah Shore recorded the song Sweet Violets in 1951, which uses the *There once was a Farmer* couplet. I have a soft spot for witty wordplay and fill-in-the-blank rhyming songs. How would your life experience mashup and retell this song?

They say she's contracted a new strain of what did you think I was going to say
It's all in your mind, and that's all for today

This phrasal mondegreen story-song sometimes ends with lines like, "You dirty young bugger, that's all for today.", "And if you think this song dirty, you're jolly well wrong." and "If you want any more you can sing it yourself," to name a few. While still using evocative imagery, in the last line, Sugra's version emphasizes and invokes the power of the mind rhyme, reality-tunnels, assumptions, innuendo, surrealism, and semantics, which implicates everyone. Where'd your mind take you?

Undulating Soundings in Time:

[0:00-0:10] Fade into Sugra's preamble, "This is called the Agriculture Song. It doesn't really make much sense to me, but I'm sure you'll understand."
[0:22-0:33] Faint campfire sizzles and waves of chuckles
[1:20-1:25] The song finishes with a giggly approving "Yeaaaaah!"
[1:33-2:01] Fades out into an impromptu, not-so-euphemistic song called *Mona*, which fittingly receives a complimentary DING! at the end from the esteemed dingers of all things DING! Robin Moorehouse

Woody Guthrie once said, "A folksinger's job is to comfort disturbed people and disturb comfortable people." You consider dreaming to be a similar job, which, you immediately reckon, is

weird to contemplate dreaming while dreaming. It feels kind of meta-lucid.

Anywho, you find yourself chopping veggies at Laughing Ladle Kitchen. You overhear Strawman Stanley misrepresent someone's statement, "You dislike onions and, in turn, soup, and yet you're making soup for the family."

"No." Reasonable Raisin counters, "I said I dislike raw onions. I love soup."

Things have gotten quite soupy here in Dreamtraillandia. You continue down the trail doing a cartwheel.

8. SHANTI STARR - PAZ

Art by Rakeup N. Wage

Recorded at the 2002 Michigan Annual Rainbow Gathering, held in the Ottawa National Forest near the town of Watersmeet, and featured on the *Michigan 2002* compilation

LISTEN:♪ 8. Shanti Starr – Paz [6:09] ♪

"Jamba is a spirit to check in with for navigating 4D chess in a fae-laden past life."
—Rainbow Trail Soundbite

Queremos paz
Queremos paz

For many but not all gatherers, the annual Rainbow gathering in the US is an omnium gatherum of individuals striving to coexist harmoniously as a community, engaged in an assortment of projects and activities, culminating with the shared intention of spending the morning of July 4th in silence and uniting in a collective prayer for peace—*OOOMMMMMM*—at High Noon. Whatever may come from that often unifying moment in time holding hands with others is, for me, peace itself, which, at the very least, helps keep hope alive...

The July 4th Variety Show at Granola Funk Theater featured a performance by Shanti entitled *Paz* (Spanish for peace). In addition to a bandshell, decoratively hung fabric, and tapestry-lined treehouse as the theater backdrop, one could surmise the stage had a woods-y tree fort-y vibe. In that era, they often drew design inspiration from the simplicity and minimalism of a chashitsu (a Japanese tea room).

Shanti played guitar and sang, Andius laid down a delectable upright bass groove, and an unknown performer played the güiro (a parallel-slitted, hollow gourd). It is a silky jam. The opening minute includes a menagerie of people making animal sounds and is among my favorite audience participation musical passages in the archive. I can't remember if people were prompted beforehand to make animal noises [0:23-1:00] or if the song's zesty licks spontaneously called it into being. Either way, I love that sequence. Several people lept off their blankets and danced beside the musicians. The song is as smooth as velvet and can free just about any closed-up heart.

"The way, 'peace is, but to follow' it's sure hard. Yeesssssss." —Rainbow Trail Soundbite

The lyrics repeated refrain, "queremos paz" ("We want peace"), continues as a clarion call, a relevant pursuit in humanity's quest to make war obsolete. PSA: Do not be fooled by haughty kingpins and tyrannical deciders.

One may view the July 4th Prayer for Peace as a revitalization of one's spirit. However Rainbow may transform in the 21st century, I wish that people continue to gather together in a moment of genuine inclusivity and union, holding hands in a prayer for peace in whatever manner is meaningful for them.

We often say 'Rest in peace,' but may we also learn to 'Live in peace' too. Although protesting in the streets and praying for peace might not end all wars, it is crucial to maintain a sense of courage and hope. Strides have been made, and war is not inevitable. Besides, courage and hope play the long game.

"Force is the weapon of the weak." —Ammon Hennessy

Peace extends beyond the absence of conflict and encompasses a range of social, political, economic, and cultural factors. In its broadest sense, peace is a state of well-being and contentment that enables individuals and communities to live fulfilling lives. One of the critical components of peace is social justice, which involves the fair and equitable distribution of resources, opportunities, and benefits. This requires addressing poverty, inequality, discrimination, patriarchy, marginalization, and climate change to create a more inclusive, diverse, and supportive society.

Like the cool shade of a willow tree, peace offers refuge from the scorching rays of turmoil. Peace resembles a tranquil garden, where the flowers of serenity bloom in abundance, their petals brushed by the gentle whispers of understanding. Peace is a respite, a pause in the frenetic pulse of existence, where the heart finds solace in the gentle rhythm of being. It's the soft lullaby of a stream, meandering through the meadows of our thoughts, washing away worry like pebbles along its path.

Peace rambles aside, this is a smokin' good tune, and we will need music—and dancing—while we work towards building a more equitable and peaceful world. The struggle continues—may peace be among the changes you wish to see in the world.

Queremos paz
Queremos paz

The Section Where Notable Audio Markings Accentuate:

[0:00-0:53] Fade into my favorite song intro in the archive, a rolling wave of animal sound effects
[1:21-1:42] The hand claps reverberate off the trees fanned adjacent to the stage. Also note: the groovy mouth percussion sounds
[2:08-2:09] A dog yelps, thus contributing, too
[2:24-3:37] "Andius on the bass" ... A funky and spacious bass solo unfolds
[3:44-3:47] Some giggles and another dog woof
[4:58-5:13] The person playing the güiro freestyles that includes an adorable shout-out to

Shanti
[6:03-6:09] Fade out into an accentuating flickering güiro flourish

   Looney Loon, with their plumage in a ponytail, reveals a youthful, unweathered face. Deep hazel eyes, set appealingly within their sockets, watch thoughtfully over their loonlets playing nearby in a pond.
   Looney's haunting call has left an impressionable mark on all who heard it, leaving a memory of visionary incantations. She swims gracefully among others.
   There's something captivating about her, perhaps it's a feeling of comfort, or perhaps it's simply her mysterious call. Nonetheless, people tend to welcome her, hoping to swim in her ripple-strokes one day.
   We hear a distant call of a conch. The moon glazes brightness.
   Looney wails for her moonlit loonlets, "AwooEEEEE!!"
   You float elsewhere, apparently along a neon green-flagged trail. Each call of the loon transforms into various colors and shapes that seemingly propel you forward.

8.8 TAHIRA & JARIS - ECSTASY

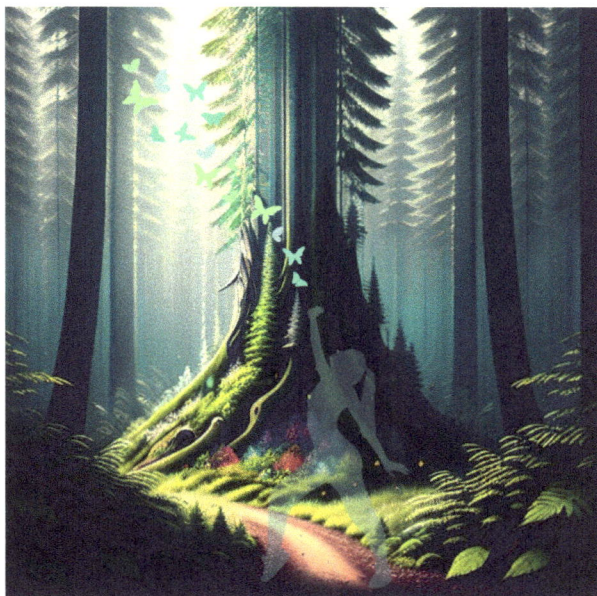

Art by Molly Sassafras

***** *Sound-Trail Diversion 4.0* *****

Recorded at the 2008 Wyoming Annual Rainbow Gathering, held in the Bridger-Teton National Forest near the town of Pinedale, and featured on the *Wyoming 2008* compilation

LISTEN:♫ [8.8 Jaris & Tahira – Ecstasy](#) [4:08] ♫

"Ecstasy orchestrates oatmeal into a scrumptious song that sings the praises of dried fruit."
—Rainbow Trail Soundbite

Recorded at Montana Camp, sometime in late June, an impromptu campfire jam with assorted people sharing and playing on each other's songs, including this scrumptious tune by Tahira and Jarvis. I love the soundbite [2:52-3:02] that giggles and claps right into an approving take on the music, "Goddamn! This is in the middle of the woods, folks!"

I'm in ecstasy
And that's okay by me
I might laugh, I might shout
I might scream, I might cry
I might change anything
But I can't deny what feels good to me
What brings me to ecstasy
What brings me love
What gives me freedom
And what brings us together as friends
We're loving and laughing and crying and singing again
I'm in ecstasy

Perplexingly, another pair of Shakespearean thespians, Ladyspice Macbeth and Hamletta Nightswoon, each wearing a velvet forest green fedora, prance by singing a familiar chant, often heard at Dinner Circle, We Art Circling:

We art circling
Circling togeth'r
We art singing
Singing our heartsong

This is family
This is unity
This is celebration
This is sacr'd

68

9. LA VIDA DOLCHE – YOU ARE MY SUNSHINE

Art by Norayaki

Recorded at the 2013 Montana Annual Rainbow Gathering, held in the Beaverhead National Forest near the town of Jackson, and featured on the *Montana 2013* compilation

LISTEN:♫ 9. La Vida Dolche – You Are My Sunshine [4:01] ♫

"Love is as above, so below" —Rainbow Trail Soundbite

You are my sunshine, my only sunshine
You make me happy when skies are gray
You'll never know, dear, how much I love you,
Please don't take my sunshine away

You Are My Sunshine is a well-known American folk song that has been covered by countless artists and remains a staple of country and folk music. The song was first recorded in 1939 by Jimmie Davis, a Louisiana politician who later became the state governor. Davis claims to have written it, but that is doubtful (many musicians back in those days erroneously claimed authorship and even went so far as to copyright songs they hadn't written), and its origins are murky at best. At any rate, the song's enduring popularity is a testament to its simple, heartfelt lyrics and catchy melody.

At the 2013 Annual Rainbow Gathering, Granola Funk built a relatively simple stage with a backdrop that had graffiti wall art 'Gfunk Revival' tagged and painted on the bandshell. They were going for the theme: "The Show Must Go On"—a throwback and shout-out homage to their early years and the hip-hop/funk band that grew out of the theater, Granola Funk Express (GFE).

La Vida Dolche performed this old chestnut at the July 4th Variety Show. They open by singing the chorus unaccompanied. I'm unsure if this group was formed for the occasion or if they were a thing. As is typical with raggle-taggle jug band/old-time/string band/busking type conglomerates, membership is fluid, and people dip in and out, which might be the case here. At any rate, about a half dozen or more of them performed together that night. I hear a resonator guitar, banjo, mandolin, fiddle, musical saw, washboard, and at least two or three lead vocalists, although everyone pretty much joined in, including the audience, on the chorus. I particularly like the folky harmonies on this track.

Despite its sunny, upbeat melody, *You Are My Sunshine's* lyrics have a melancholic tinge. The song speaks of lost love and the pain of separation but also expresses a deep sense of hope and the belief that love will eventually triumph over sadness and despair. The song is as American as apple pie, and I'd be hard-pressed to find someone who hasn't heard it within its borders. I doubt I could find someone who dislikes it, but I'm sure that person exists, hanging out at the smug Hot Take Saloon. La Vida Dolche's version is among my favorite recordings from that gathering and the song itself. A piquant bit is when they swap moonshine for sunshine on the final chorus, adding an ambiguous element.

Excellent version—I give La Vida Dolche's *You Are My Sunshine* 5-stars

You are my moonshine, my only moonshine
You make me happy when skies are gray
You'll never know, dear, how much I need you,
Please don't take my moonshine away

Like Waves In The Soundglass, So Are The Stamps of Time:

[0:00-0:24] Fade into a sunny shine of a capella-ness
[0:26-0:40] The washboard flicks and flicks again, which sounds like a baseball card in a bike tire
[0:41-0:42] DING!
[0:59-1:00] A thrusting DING!
[1:16-1:17] A mighty DING! turns frowns upside down
[2:24-2:42] It's subtle and requires close listening, but a musical saw intertwines through the mix
[3:33-3:34] That howl is well-timed and we'll-played
[3:35-4:01] Fade out into a capella-ness 2.0 with alternate lyrics, and of course, for good measure, we get a final climatic DING!

You glissade through a meadow and look up. A cloud passes over in letter shapes that form words into a phrase, "Folk music reversed becomes cisum klof."

Precipitously, an Observant Owl swoops right over your head and drops a piece of birch bark on your lap that has a poem scratched into it:

~ Love's Mighty Crest ~

A sonorous voice as fair as a forest stream evokes notions of gleam
Melodies trickle and flow autonomously in rippling exotic stare
Enticing the big dipper to scoop amongst the scoop of scoops
To cleanse our searching thirst, which yearns for the soothing muse

What we seek and what we find is still the eternal love in patterns knot
There is no secret how to unchain our hearts, which we keep hidden and locked
So we may soar on cherub wings, in clouds of pearls unleashed in skies of thought
Embroidered in silky hopes and velvety wishes woven to still do the dishes

Smiles upon smiles unmasked by the mysterious and ancient call of the loon
Sending ripples that swoon towards the moon, which bestows life's treasure chest
Safe harbor for our undiscovered twists and the whispy looms that do turn
Yet unveiled in our closet of dreams, we clasp for the joys of love's mighty crest

10. OWL NIGHT LAKE III

Art by Numinous 'Night Owl' Nobleoak

Recorded at the 2019 Wisconsin Annual Rainbow Gathering, held in the Chequamegon–Nicolet National Forest near the town of Iron River, and featured on the *Wisconsin 2019* compilation

LISTEN:♫ 10. Owl Night Lake III [2:22] ♫

"Gathering of beings from all corners of the galaxy, a Rainbow gathering is."
—Owl the Wise

Early in Seed Camp, I took a walk near Steelhead Lake to record some natural soundscapes. I stopped approximately 25 meters from the lake's shoreline and hit record. Crickets stridulate their courting song. Peepers prance their own mating frequency. Meanwhile, some barred owls have some things to say as well, perhaps engaged in the throngs of love, looking to propose (Barred Owls are monogamous and typically mate for life).

Owl hoots are a distinctive and recognizable sound often associated with the nighttime forest. The hoots themselves can vary in pitch, tone, and duration, depending on the species of owl and the context in which they are communicating. In some cases, owl hoots may be a form of territorial signaling, with male owls using their hoots to establish their presence and deter other males from encroaching on their territory. Hoots can also be a means of communication between owls of the same species, with males and females using different hoots to signal their location and establish contact with each other. Some owl species are recognized for emitting distinctive "mating calls," using a series of hoots, trills, or other vocalizations to attract a mate.

Barred Owls have the fabled "Who cooks for you? Who cooks for you-all?" call, which, I quite like those lyrics—it's like a talkin' blues or some wry social commentary folk song. Although not considered a songbird, I find their call quite musical.

In addition to their communication functions, owl hoots can also serve as a way of identifying different species of owls. Each species has its own unique hoot pattern and pitch, which can help birdwatchers and naturalists identify and distinguish between different species in the wild. In mythology worldwide, owls have been portrayed in various ways, but they are often associated with mystery, wisdom, and the supernatural.

This recording exemplifies how various species use the airwaves, finding the optimal frequency to make their voice heard and understood. I like how the reverberating call and response hoots between the owl's pan across the stereo imaging, which you can listen to more so with a good pair of headphones.

I sure do love the night-time sounds that abound in the summertime up north, eh.

Brief Time-Stretches of Post-Merging of Sound:

[0:00-0:07] Fade into crickets, frogs, and a worthy hooting question: "Who cooks for you?

Who cooks for you-all?"

[0:20-1:27] Reverberating sequences: "Who cooks for you? Who cooks for you-all?"

[1:39-1:51] We hear an audible hooty response that feels as if it pans mainly to the right channel

[2:05-2:22] Fade out into more calls stating that kitchens seek help

The mixed and expansive woodland was a magnificent spectacle, teaming with an abundance of life. Towering pine, hickory, and juniper trees competed for space in the uppermost branches. At the same time, intermittent sunbeams penetrated through, casting a mosaic of light and shade upon the fertile floor below, where young saplings flourished. The uppermost branches were still, while the lower levels were relatively uniform, save for the occasional burst of vibrant flowers in secluded corners. A chorus of sounds echoed throughout the forest from its diverse inhabitants, with insects and animals creating a wild and boisterous symphony that overshadowed the gentle splashing of trout in the nearby stream. Meanwhile, Brave Bear stretches using a tree as a scratching post. She plops back down, yawns, and then ponders: "The journey of a thousand dreams begins with a single stretch."

You mosey on as water flows to the sea, swimming along a light blue-n-pink-flagged trail.

10.7 ANGELA - OM SHALOM SALAM

Art by Prarie Meadow

***** *Sound-Trail Diversion 5.0* *****

Recorded at the 2002 Michigan Annual Rainbow Gathering, held near the town of Watersmeet in the Ottawa National Forest, and featured on the *Michigan 2002* compilation

LISTEN:♫ 10.7 Angela - Om Shalom Salem [8:13] ♫

"Pot Village needs haiku pudding for a meadow mashup."—Rainbow Trail Soundbite

Om Shalom Salam
Om Shalom Salam

Recorded at Jerusalem Camp on the evening of July 3rd during a night of song sharing. Such delightful music was made around the campfire that night—chants, folk, reggae, religious, and secular songs. This piece, led by Angela on the harp, embodies peace in song (listen for that deep bowed upright bass pulsations played by Andius). Shalom means "peace" in Hebrew, and salam means "peace" in Arabic. Om is a sacred sound in Hinduism and is considered the sound of the universe, the original vibration. All sounds lead to Om, and may such vibrations bring peace to all.

Om Shalom Salam
Om Shalom Salam

The Fuchsiarap Oneohsevenphyllus, colloquially known as Rap 107, is a rare, medium-sized plant exclusive to planet Earth and blooms in late summer, knowing that cleanup begins when you arrive. It features broad needle leaves, typically in forest green, and produces substantial flowers in shades of summery lemon and dazzling pink, especially when we have community fires only. While these plants grow in small clusters to optimize community engagement, they are straightforward to maintain and regulate, much like a slit trench latrine. Thus, they prefer to camp together in established neighborhoods. When you wash your hands with it to protect our health, it can provide a salubrious and energizing effect. As a defense mechanism, the Fuchsiarap Oneohsevenphyllus imitates the appearance of a Packitinia Packitoutus plant, whereby both help to keep soaps out of streams. It practices radical inclusion and consent. Water currents aid in dispersing their seeds for reproduction, and once pollinated, they produce sizable and delectable fruits of potable water. Join us for a Silent Contemplation & Prayer for Peace. Please respect the silence from dawn to noon when the children's parade arrives at the main meadow. We Love You~

11. DANJHEL – COSAS BELLAS

Art by Uri & Faraway Lookinyereye

Recorded at the 2005 Panama Rainbow Gathering, held near the town of Boquete, and featured on the *Panama 2005* compilation

LISTEN: ♫ 11. Danjhel – Cosas Bellas [3:42] ♫

"Rumor has grit, pack it in means to pack it out through the outta here trail"
—Rainbow Trail Soundbite

Ahora ve, camina los bosques, piensas en cosas bellas y enamórate...

Cosas Bellas (Beautiful Things), a song of deep longing, complete with alluring lyrics, was recorded late in the evening, with only a few of us gathered around a small fire in the gathering's main kitchen. The symbiosis between the song and the background nighttime forest sounds is the bee's knees for me. Couple that with sweet vocal harmony by Gaby (who also kindly provided the lyrics and English translation).

Danjhel is a talented Panamanian singer-songwriter. We had a few recording sessions at the 2005 and 2006 Panamian gatherings. Both gatherings were magical, small and quaint, with great company, music, food, smiles, and laughter. Invariably, Panama's beautifully lush and diverse landscape spread across its curvy isthmus layout, and the kindheartedness and community-mindedness of its people indeed planted the seeds for marvelous things to follow.

That night, in 2005, most had gone to sleep, and anyone who has been in a Rainbow kitchen in the wee hours can relate when a beautiful song gets played, and everyone who has been staring at dancing embers and two smoky sticks pretending to be a fire, thinking it might be time for bed, suddenly finds themselves swept up in a gorgeous melody, which undulates like a blessing, granting us to just be in the moment, together, as one.

Once in a while, such moments get recorded, and *Cosas Bellas* is a quintessential example of late-night Muse-infused music-making magic and harmony~

Tú no tienes la sospecha y te llevo en una estrella
Viendo las cosas hermosas en el verso de una prosa
Y te cuento que en los mares los delfines tienen pares
Hasta el alba es más perfecta solo cuando así la miras tu
Oh tu

Pero yo
Llevo un mundo en guerra
Y jamás quisiera que lo vieras tu
Ahora ve, camina los bosques
Piensas en cosas bellas y sonríete

Ni siquiera te imaginas y te llevo en una cima
Respirando el aire puro, contemplando nuestro imperio
Y te tomo de la mano caminando por los prados
Es la noche más calmada solo cuando en ella estás tu
Oh tu

Pero yo
Vivo un mundo en guerra
Y jamás quisiera que lo vieras tu
Ahora ve, camina los bosques
Piensas en cosas bellas y enamórate

Yo no cambio el pensamiento
De tu verde sentimiento
Extraviarte en la ventana
Solo pensando en mi

Yo no cambio el dulce aliento
Que me trae tu fresca boca
Yo seré el que se desboca
Y en la senda se acomoda a ti
Claro que si

Y aun te cuento que en los valles
Se oye el canto de las aves
De la forma más preciosa
Solo cuando lo acompañas tu
Oh tu

~ Beautiful Things ~
You are not suspecting it, and I take you on a star
Seeing the beautiful things in the verse of a prose
And I tell you that in the seas, the dolphins have pairs
Even the dawn is more perfect only when you look at it that way
Oh you

But I
I have a world at war
And I would never want you to see it
Now go, walk in the woods
Think of beautiful things and smile

You can't even imagine it, and I take you to a peak
Breathing the fresh air, contemplating our empire
And I take you by the hand, walking through the meadows
It is the calmest night only when you are in it
oh you

But I
I live in a world at war
And I would never want you to see it
Now go, walk in the woods
Think of beautiful things and fall in love
I do not change the thought
Of your green feeling
Getting lost in the window
Just thinking of me

I don't change the sweet breath
That your fresh mouth brings

I'll be the one that runs wild
And on the path adapts to you
Yes, of course
And I still tell you that in the valleys
You hear the singing of birds
In the most precious way
Only when you accompany it
Oh you

<u>The Garden Snippets of Dreamy Delights:</u>

[0:00-0:15] Fade into a birdsong transition to symbiotic guitar strums and crickets
[0:40-0:42] Sweet accompanying vocal; weaves and blends throughout
[1:00-2:00] In my view, such a great mix of song and crickets, so this timestamp is arbitrary other than to say "oh-la-la"
[3:19-3:21] "Ahh, bonita." Indeed
[3:22-3:43] Fade out into a *tweener*: Distant sound of the Chiriquí Nuevo River and an unidentified bird (I tried to identify the species via BirdNET and Merlin Bird ID apps to no avail, can you?)

The moon shines as bright as the goodness in your heart. Camp Gobbledygook just dumpster dove a bunch of everything bagels. But they have nothing to put on them. Something has got to give, they think. The universe blessed us with everything, but we have nothing, yet we still have something, everything, and nothing. We should be content, they reckon. Maybe the moonlight makes us as silly as a flat earther searches for the edge. We're making much ado about nothing, as sometimes happens while dreaming. Be that as it may, one of them, Hemlock Hansel, strums a lonesome blues progression on a resonator guitar and sings:

~ Blue Moonlight Blues ~

Why does love have to wish to be had?
Why does love have to wish to be had?
For when the heartaches, the moon looks sad

Must our promenade persist in fear?
Must our promenade persist in fear?
For the twilight cries, it's all right here

Take a stone and embrace the moonlight
Take a stone and embrace the moonlight
The union of this ever so bright

Here is here and there is there until
Here is here and there is there until
We harbor the soul safe, calm, and still

11.23 NĀDA BINDU – MYSTERY

Art by Big Quark

***** Sound-Trail Diversion 6.0 *****

Recorded at the 2001 Idaho Annual Rainbow Gathering, held in the Boise National Forest near the town of Stanley, and featured on the *Leftovers III: The MiniDisc Years 2000-2009* compilation

LISTEN:♫ 11.23 Nāda Bindu – Mystery [5:19] ♫

"So you sang everlasting tent blossoms with an immense lightline?"
—Rainbow Trail Soundbite

Mystery's origin story is a bit of a mystery (hence, the title given). The performance comes from a night of music from Nāda Bindu at Zipolite/Deva Diner. The group explored various North African and Middle Eastern musical styles. I was fortunate to record them at several gatherings in the early 2000s. Always a good time.

Robby plays oud and sings lead vocals. Sam plays clarinet and percussion. Carlito plays darbuka. Others join in on backup vocals. It's a mesmeric groove replete with sweet harmonies.

In the mid-1990s, Robby learned many songs throughout North Africa and the Middle East. This one is among them. However, seeing how memory is as slippery as a banana peel in a bucket of lard, he suspects he learned it as part of a Nubian frame drum song in upper Egypt.

Depending on your listener's contour, the lyrics' importance may vary. For me, this is often dependent on mood and musical style. At times, even when the lyrics are comprehended, their meaning remains shrouded in ambiguity, where the essence imbued within the song ascends beyond the mere confines of lyrical content. Music connects the dots of communication in ways language cannot.

Phonetically, the lyrics transliterate as follows: *wi sama hin noba*. The text is possibly Nobiin, a language belonging to the Nilo-Saharan phylum, specifically the Northern Nubian branch. Approximately half a million Nubians reside along the Nile River in southern Egypt and northern Sudan, where they speak the language. Considering the various dialects, I wasn't able to unveil anything nor find a native speaker who could assist.

In Arabic, *wi* means *and*. In ancient texts, *Noba* refers to the Noba people, who migrated to the region in the 4th century following the decline of the Meroitic kingdom. The Noba community spoke a Nilo-Saharan language as the precursor to Old Nubian. Old Nubian was primarily used in religious writings dated between the 8th and 15th centuries. In the epochs of classical antiquity and preceding the 4th century, the region known as Nubia garnered its appellation as Kush. *Hin* means *when*. The term *Sama* denotes the act of listening.

Or perhaps the lyrics are an amalgam of the two languages.

Nevertheless, accurately translating the lyrics remains elusive and likely an uneducated and futile exercise on my part. However, perhaps the act of listening through devotion is meaningful enough.

Whether it's the melody, rhythm, lyrics, timbre, or what have you, the impact of a song is dependent upon the *ears* of the beholder, colored by experience, temperament, and taste.

The origin of *Mystery* remains as mysterious as life itself.

Timeless Turtle sits on a driftwood nestled along a lake shore and queries, "I am always dreaming. I must always be awake. The feet I strut will soon turn left. What am I?"

o
( )
|

Author note here's a clue: I am what I am

11.5 ~O~O~O~O~O~

Art by Upik/Warehouse Work & Grata Domum

Recorded at the 2021 Pennsylvania Prism Rainbow Gathering, held in the Allegheny National Forest near the town of Ridgway, and featured on the *Pennsylvania Prism 2021* compilation

LISTEN: ♫ 11.50. Tom & Joosh - Campfire Strings I [4:20] ♫

"The mapeth is not the t'rrit'ry." —Rainbow Trail Soundbite

Late-night sitting around the campfire, an impromptu instrumental guitar duo spontaneously unfolded. I sit directly between Tom and Joosh, positioning my microphone equidistant, which bestows rich stereo imaging. This sonic sense becomes more pronounced when listening through headphones. Together, the strings intertwine and flow like two adjoining streams. *Campfire Strings I* is as soft as moss and as smooth as clay. ~O~O~O~O~O~

Before we conclude the Campfire Inter(planetary)mission Safety Meeting (CISM), and you continue to drift on down thee ol' trail, the theater of the mind presents a joke:

A traveler walks into a dream and hands the Sandman a fistful of dirt. The Sandman smiles cordially and says, "Welcome to the wanderlust land of REMarkable adventures!" and gives them time for change.

12. LYDIYAH & SHANDA PANDA – UMOJAH

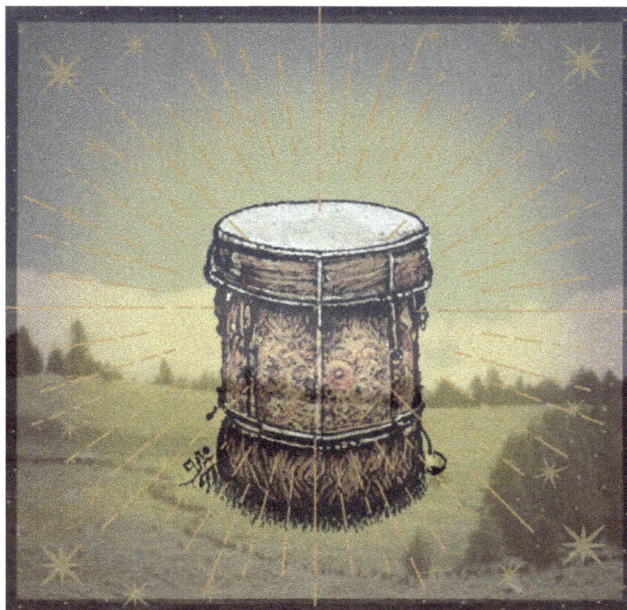

Art by Wynd Rithum

Recorded at the 2000 Montana Annual Rainbow Gathering held in the Beaverhead National Forest near the town of Jackson and featured on the *Leftovers III: The MiniDisc Years 2000-2009* compilation

LISTEN:♫ 12. Lydiyah & Shanda Panda – Most High [6:03] ♫

"Interconnectedness is the zuzu of non-locality" —Rainbow Trail Soundbites

The concept of the Most High typically refers to a divine entity that unveils the universe and is found in many different religious and spiritual traditions. And on this night, sometime around the summer solstice, perhaps even the summer solstice, memory seems to forget what it knows. Memory is like a magic trick—you have to spell it out.

Nāda Bindu Camp invited and hosted an evening of campfire chant and song. Their camp was tucked away down a winding trail deep into the woods. Several dozen people were sitting around the fire when I arrived. Such a fantastic night, brimming with love, mystery, and magic, it was.

I had recorded my first music at Rainbow only a few days earlier, so this was my first night making a campfire recording. I had no clue what I was doing, where to place myself, or what kind of music to expect.

Umojah is a word derived from Swahili and is often associated with unity and togetherness. Nowadays, umojah extends beyond the African diaspora and has influenced movements for social justice and equality around the world. It also represents solidarity and the strength that can be found in coming together, emphasizing the value of collective effort and cooperation in order to achieve common objectives and improve the lives of individuals and communities.

Inspired by the word and what it represents, Lydia, who sings lead vocal, wrote *Umojah* in 1999. Shanda Panda accompanies on backup vocal, and many others join in and sing along. A mishmash of people played various sorts of percussion. *Umojah* illustrates the kind of Rainbow campfire sing-along and chants commonly heard at Rainbow gatherings.

If memory pulls a rabbit from the hat, this is also a rare field recording of mine where I set the mic on a small tripod and joined in on percussion. I played an udu drum (a clay pot vessel from Nigeria that has become widely used by percussionists worldwide) I had inexplicably brought to the gathering. Gosh knows how it made it through that gathering without cracking. Various techniques can be employed to alter the pitch when played with one's hands. You can hear its deep watery, and cavernous sound—*dooooop!*—throughout the track.

The hit record and chance microphone placement approach worked in this case. The rotund circumjacent vocals and percussion immerse the aural space, soothing my heart upon every listen. We became one through music. I love the booming bass beats and the interweaving of vocals (and the scat/mouth music *dun dun dun* vocal bit)—an exemplary moment of unity.

Most High, Most High
We become one
Mother, Father
We become one
Children, Grandchildren
We become one
Roots of Gaia
We become one
Holy Zion
We become one

Heaven's blessings are here to stay
Realizations bring them here today
Wake up the Ancestors, help us on our way
Our visions walking bring a new day

Free up your sorrow
Free up your joy
The world's emotion
Has gone to devotion
Of the Most High, Most High
We become one
Through the Most High, Most High
We become one

No more struggle, no more scorn
People's hearts no longer torn
Earth Mother shall ever be reborn
As a love manifest, we become one

A soul's journey has brought us here
The time to gather is right now, right here
Release expectations, release all fear

For the Most High Jah, our hearts must be sincere
The Most High Jah, our sight must be clear

Free up your sorrow
Free up your joy
The world's emotion
Has gone to devotion
Of the Most High, Most High
We become one
Through the Most High, Most High
We become one

Audio Notes Awaken:

[0:00-0:22] Fade into chant refrain and a beat that is one though the drums be many
[0:23] In a rare occurrence, the author has the mic placed on a small tripod and is playing an udu (a clay drum) that you can hear throughout if you listen closely
[0:38-0:42] Love the background reverberating wail that ripples through the trees, uplifting the groove
[1:31-1:37] Udu plosives become slightly more audible
[2:23-2:33] Nice weaving of voices between Lydiyah and Shanda
[4:07-4:10] Another background woot-woot makes an impression
[5:25-6:03] Fade out into a mandolin trickle, some background woots, and "I love that song." Yeah, me too; it's smashing

You're sipping coffee at Camp Sir Cumference Round Table. Dilatante Doober talks about helping with the dishes, but his words sail to the land of the dubious. Wherewithal Wynne means

business when they chop wood, carry water. Shapeshifting Sammy transformed into this sentence. Potential Pollyanna advises, "When you have no spoons to give, there's always a fork to take." Labyrinthine Lucy flips multiple pancakes, holding eight spatulas in one hand while juggling three sticks of butter in the other. Halcyon Hank is as happy as a mud wrestler in a mud pit. Supercilious Suzie sloganly boasts, "I change, so you don't have to." Impiety Isla uses soap to clean cast iron skillets. Fugacious Fenyx considers life a gift. Eloquent Emerie ponders, "In the delicate ballet of reality, as the orchestra of life unfolds its ethereal melodies, we find ourselves humbled witnesses to the grand tapestry of cosmic wonders, forever awed by the interplay of light and shadow that paints the canvas of our journey."

Nearby, Curious Clementine stares at a patch of moss with deep gazing eyes harboring the patience of an ancient oak. A mushroom turns to them and says, "Imagine a vibrant portal at the trunk of the sacred tree. Gravity pulls at you with such force that resistance is meaningfully meaningless. You soar on an infinite carpet of luminous note vibrations. Despite this sudden change, there's an unusual beauty in this weird world of cosmic oneness. In the distance, you hear the songs and growls of creatures that seem familiar zip by you, altering the pitch like the Doppler effect. You can see seeking creatures, playful creatures, and what appear to be pensive creatures. With careful rationing, your supplies should last for a while as you embark on an extraordinary journey through light and sound. By being cautious, having backup plans, exerting solid yet flexible planning, and recognizing the inherent Rashomon effect omnipresent in the human experience, you'll be able to explore this realm to its fullest potential."

However, as quick as the blink of this life, you find yourself whisked away to a meadow serving food at Main Circle. You scoop rice with a ladle from a large pot, carefully not touching the ladle thing to the person's bowl thing, and you proceed to drop about a cup worth into their bowl— plop! This experience feels quite good. Your potential contains multitudes.

12.3 ROCKER T - RAINBOW COUNTRY

Art by Voy 'Poary Huffleg' Age

***** *Sound-Trail Diversion 7.0* *****

Recorded at the 2003 Utah Annual Rainbow Gathering, held in the Bridger Teton National Forest near the town of Mt View, Wyoming, and featured on the *Utah 2003: Leftovers III* compilation

LISTEN:♫ 12.3 Rocker T - Rainbow Country [5:37] ♫

"The goal of vibration is to sherpa the skynet of complexity rather than boil greywater."
—Rainbow Trail Soundbite

We're going to that Rainbow country
And we're moving to that promised land

It's July 2nd at Devapoo / Kick-a-Deva / Clandestino / [insert whatever-name-you-remember-if-you-were-there-or-even-if-you-weren't] Kitchen. Rocker T stopped by with a crew of musicians to perform around the campfire. We savored delectable baked zuzu confections, like strawberry cheesecake and chocolate truffles, to cookies and brownies, accompanied by fragrant chai and strongly brewed coffee, while the music promised to deliver an exquisite and flavorsome jamboree. Dopamine was released in great abundance.

T and I met earlier in the day and planned on doing a campfire recording session, as per tradition from previous gatherings. Rocker T and musical companions unfurled one gem after another, crafting a resplendent evening of music adorned with community-affirming exultations and beautiful vibes, evoking a sense of awesomeness in its purest essence.

Dacher Keltner writes in his book *Awe: The New Science of Everyday Wonder and How It Can Transform Your Life,* "Awe is the feeling of being in the presence of something vast that transcends your current understanding of the world." Apply this notion to music and that night, elucidating the indescribable splendor of a collective campfire serenade.

Love~ Joy~ Bliss~ Awe~

Rainbow Country is an upbeat rootsy amalgam of Rainbow reggae and heartsong, a classic gathering song if there ever was one, melodically engrossing, replete with catchy lyrical phrasing—*Boom!*

I'm going to bless my temple
And be the best that I can be
I'm going to shine like a shining star
For all of the angels to see

Thespian alert This time, it's Windytarp Wordsworth, who takes a break from fire trolling and soliloquies a version of the chant, The Earth is our Moth'r:

The earth is our moth'r, we wilt taketh careth of h'r
The earth in our moth'r, we wilt taketh careth of h'r

Ho yanna ho yanna ho yon yon,
Ho yanna ho yanna ho yon yon
H'r sacr'd did grind we walketh upon, with ev'ry stepeth we taketh

The sky is our fath'r, we shall taketh careth of that gent
His sacr'd air we breatheth in, with ev'ry breath we taketh

Ho yanna ho yanna ho yon yon,
Ho yanna ho yanna ho yon yon
H'r sacr'd did grind we walketh upon, with ev'ry stepeth we taketh

13. PODANK – BEERNANEARNEAR

Art by Suddenlee 'Snow Drift' Sawseepan

Recorded at the 2003 Utah Annual Rainbow Gathering, held in the Bridger Teton National Forest near the town of Mt View, Wyoming, and featured on the *Utah 2003* compilation

LISTEN:♫ 13. PoDank – Beernanearnear [3:50] ♫

"Supercalifragilisticexpialidociouspockettrade" —Rainbow Trail Soundbite

Field Guide to Field Recording a String Band in a Snow Blizzard [2nd Edition] by Fryin' Pan Yeti, An excerpt - -

Introduction

Field recording in a blizzard in the mountains is an exhilarating and challenging endeavor that allows you to capture the unique soundscape of a string band in a winter storm in a breathtaking natural setting. However, it requires careful planning, specialized equipment, and a strong appreciation for stormy weather. This field guide will provide you with essential tips and techniques for successful field recording in these harsh conditions.

1. Preparation

Before heading out to record string bands in a blizzard in the mountains, it's crucial to be well-prepared:

A. Research:
- Study the weather forecast and wood pile conditions
- Choose a cozy campfire with easy access to music
- Identify potential songs and plan singalong routes

B. Equipment:

- Invest in high-quality vibes, including banjos, guitar, fiddle, and upright bass
- Dress in warm, layered clothing with waterproof gear
- Carry extra flexibility and memory cards

C. Safety & Treats:

- Camping in a neighborhood can enhance safety during a blizzard by providing extra support and assistance if needed; check in with those around you to ensure they have everything they need to stay wardm and dry
- Inform someone that you have chocolate to share, including salted dark and caramel
- Consider sharing said chocolate; it'll alleviate the cold by some measure

2. Recording Techniques

When you're out in the blizzard, follow these techniques to capture the best possible audio:
A. Wind & String Management:

- Use a lucky mojo on your microphone to reduce wind noise and increase string crispness
- Position the microphone to minimize exposure to troll polls

B. Snow and Ice Sounds:

- Seek out areas with different snowy string textures, such as clawhammer, flat, or fingerpicking.
- Record the sound of snowflakes that reverberate as they approach the upright bass.

C. Ambience:

- Capture the overall ambiance by recording campfire flickers for extended periods.
- Experiment with microphone placement to capture the subtle nuances of the string band's soundscape in hopes you can create evocative recordings that transport listeners to the heart of a string band in a winter storm

*To read more, find Fryin' Pan Yeti's best-selling field guidebook wherever you get your guidebooks.

In *Gathering Sounds*, we traversed through a snow blizzard recording. We revisit that night with PoDank's *Beernanearnear*. I did not set out to make a field recording in Arctic-type conditions. I had never even considered it before. I had finished delivering some fresh baked goods and was making my way back to our kitchen. I passed by a small campfire, and some familiar people I had met at previous gatherings were playing music around a campfire. A few others sat nearby, huddled and cuddled in a puddle. The warmth of the music and fire made us almost forget we were standing in over a foot of snow. The snow continued to fall heavily like a child frantically shaking a snow globe.

As I understand, last I reached out to them, PoDank—as is often the case with bands—was a short-lived outfit. Still, even so, in their home state of Oklahoma, their captivating live performances left a lasting impression and are quite legendary in some circles. They were also well-loved at Rainbow that year, playing rousing performances at various campfires, as witnessed by the energetic and nifty picking on *Beernanearnear*.

Imagine mashing up the zaniness of Ween, the dexterous picking of Foggy Mountain Boys, bits of talkin' blues, and old-time folk styles. Add a punk as fuck attitude, and you have PoDank. This song exemplifies their extraordinary talent; even a snowstorm—*The Hoedown in the Blowdown!*—couldn't slow them down.

The lyrics and the swirling picking suggest the presence of a beernananear and what might have prompted the creation of this song. Whatever the inspiration may be, *Beernanearnear* never ceases to put a pep in my step.

Beernanearnear
Beernanearnear
Beernanearnear
Beernanearnear
Beernanearnear

Catch me where I'm fallin'
Say that you can't stay
Catch me where I'm fallin'
Our love is a brighter day
At least that's what I say

The Sound Also Awakens (With Notes):

[0:00-1:20] Fade into an extended punkgrass (PoDank's term) opening jam of campfire delight
[1:22-1:32] The two vocalists have a knack for exquisitely playing their voices off of each other
[2:37-3:07] Thumpy bass thumps give the kind of thumps a bass is supposed to thump
[3:38-3:50] Fade out into whistling applause and "That song is called Beernanearnear."

A venerable ash tree leans in close to you and murmurs through its shimmering leaves, "Music fathoms the trail of song where one arrives at the intersection of syncopation and swing."

Inexplicably, you find yourself chopping wood at Big Time PSA Bakery & Cafe. Someone unravels an ancient scroll made out of hemp, requests everyone's attention, and reports in a yodeling waddle: "Ahem, in preparation for cleanup.... Pack up all your trash and bring it to the appropriate staging areas. Dismantle and disappear your encampment. Vanish ALL traces. Fire Rocks scattered, ashes cold and buried, pits filled in. Latrines and compost holes are covered over. String and twine get removed from tree limbs. Hardened ground gets aerated with tools for future root growth and moisture catch. Help with recycling. All trash is removed. Please take trash with you. Every bag or load helps. Where everyone helps, the effort is made easier. When an area is clear and clean, then NATURALIZE! Scatter logs, branches, leaves, and duff to disappear trails and camps and renew forest habitats. H2O systems and latrine tops are removed and cleaned for future use. Fully dismantle ramps and bridges. Steep places are water-barred to prevent erosion. Transport as many riders as possible to aid our travels. Treat local folks with kindness. Drive safely and share this love wherever you go."

Meanwhile, an Elegant Elf named Baeleath Farylark, sits on a giant fern and mashes up a ballad motif by inserting a nursery rhyme-y chorus, as remixers are wont to do. Baeleath sings unaccompanied:

~ Duff's Liturgical Ballad No.701 ~

1 My eyes rise to a harlequin sunrise
The tattered morning engulfed in a bruised sigh
I pray to the plump cherubs way up high
How long, O, how long must I be cast aside?

Heart comes in, heart goes out
Some with duff, some without
Thus it goes, seed to sprout
Some with cheer some with pout

2 My memories claw an old painted face
For wrinkles are the scars of experience
I say to the heavens that command brilliance
How long, O how long must I endure the chase?

Heart comes in, heart goes out
Some with duff, some without
Thus it goes, seed to sprout
Some with cheer, some with pout

Suddenly, you're lying comfortably in your tent, feeling cozy, the distant drum circle lulls you to sleep. You wake up living to dream and dreaming to live. You do-si-do in through the corner swirl, and you shake it all about. That's what this dream is all about!

14. RAGGEDY ANN − MAKE BELIEVE

Art by Bake Melieve

Recorded at the 2008 Wyoming Annual Rainbow Gathering, held in the Bridger-Teton National Forest near the town of Pinedale, and featured on the *Leftovers III: The MiniDisc Years 2000-2009* compilation

LISTEN:♫14. Raggedy Ann − Make Believe [3:55] ♫

"I am a moist road spirit from nowhere" —Rainbow Trail Soundbite

Make-believe is the act of pretending or imagining things that are not real (so they say). It is a common activity for children and is often seen as a way for them to develop their creativity and problem-solving skills. Children may engage in make-believe by inventing and playing games, creating imaginary worlds, or acting out scenarios. O, how lamentable it is when the beginner's mind fades away, pretending as if make-believe isn't what we're doing all the time anyhow.

This is your daydream speaking....
That's right, I can read your minds,
And that's exactly what I was thinking
Is this for real...
Is this a dream?
Can you then tell me thee answer
or the origin of the light that shines from inside
or what really lies tied beneath these seams?
Well, I can,
And I've tried,
But through time you've unlearned the language of my slumberland
Now I'm tired of trying to wind the key
On your grown-up and rusted-shut music box mind

The Spoken Word/Open Mic Night was hosted by Diamond Dave on July 3rd at Popcorner Camp. This event also coincided with a memorial for a friend of many, Mark Sparks, who had crossed the Rainbow Bridge shortly before the Wyoming gathering. As he was known to have a sweet tooth, we made preparations to hand out hundreds of s'more fixings to celebrate his life. We passed the word down the trail to "bring your own stick" (BYOS).

It turned out to be a warm and cozy night of song, story, and poetry. A balm for the aggressive force used by Forest Service LEOs hours earlier, the intimate open mic provided comfort to those affected by the excessive use of pepper spray bullets by the cops following the arrest of a man in possession of a relatively small amount of cannabis[5]. In addition to s'mores, Popcorner prepared popcorn and chai. There are several recordings

---

5 The incident gained some national attention. Check out the documentary We Love You to view footage of how things transpired.

from that night included in the *Sounds from the Rainbow* archive. Also, to find a genre list, namely to help locate a particular style of recording, visit soundsfromtherainbow.org/genres.

We had gathered around a campfire on the edge of a meadow, with a mix of pine, spruce, fir, and aspen groves surrounding us. Everyone did the 1-2-3 call out, "WERE OVER HERE!" notifying gatherers in the distance that we were set to begin. People were encouraged to share an A Side and a B Side.

Raggedy Ann guided us through the looking glass with an exquisite story examining the perception of reality, the self, and the power of imagination. Using vivid wordplay, Raggedy Ann cast a magic spell over the audience. She transported us to a dream-filled world of wonder and mystery. Her performance was a masterclass in storytelling, as she skillfully wove together words into metaphors to create a mesmerizing narrative that captivated us from beginning to end. Raggedy Ann's use of tone, inflection, and gesture brought the story-poem to life. Each turn of phrase felt real and tangible, captivating us from beginning to end. The secret behind rekindling the beginner's mind is recognizing that everything we do is, in essence, an act of make-believe.

> *We are the glimmer and the glean*
> *We are the scissors and the seam*
> *We play things*
> *We can be anything*
> *We can be the twinkle of eyes or the smile on your face*
> *We can be the last trace of the chalk hopscotch*
> *That the rains never seem to erase*
> *We are the color of bubbles and the shape of stars*
> *We can be created out of whatever have you,*
> *And wherever it happens that you are,*
> *And so you see my human dream beings,*
> *The answer is not something that can be explained or seen*
> *The answer is always what you make-believe*

Audio Examinations In Dreamtime's Make-Believe:

[0:00-0:08] Fade into "Hello, lovelies" is met with a response "Hey Beautiful" and "Hey,

Raggity Annie."

[0:14-0:18] "I can read your minds." is also met with a response, "Ah, good."

[0:45-1:00] The distant drums pulse almost as if they're not there except when you choose to hone in on them

[1:15-3:50] A violin or cello (?) sits nearby, subtly warming up or intently adding make-believed bowed accents

[3:45-3:55] Fades out into what you choose to make-believe

Regal Raven has omniscient eyes as dark as a cave, looks magnificent perched on a Douglas Fir limb, and speaks with guidance: "Inclusivity is essential in creating a positive and welcoming environment for everyone. Regardless of your age, gender, ethnicity, faith, physical abilities, or any other aspect of your identity, you are a valid and valued human. We embrace diversity and celebrate the unique perspectives and experiences that each individual brings to the wood pile. With care and respect, we strive to create a safe and supportive space for all."

With that stem drop, Regal Raven takes flight, direction unknown. You float-stroll along a Rainbow-flagged trail.

14.4 STILTS - GUITAR & MELODICA

Art by Chugga Chugga Chugga Chugga Choo Choo

***** *Sound-Trail Diversion 8.0* *****

Recorded at the 2000 Montana Annual Rainbow Gathering, held in the Beaverhead National Forest near the town of Jackson, and featured on the *Montana 2000* compilation

LISTEN:♫ 14.4 Stilts - Guitar & Melodica [1:50] ♫

"Don't touch your thing hot pan now, Myles Mooniverse. Water camp needs wavey, watery words!" —Rainbow Trail Soundbite

A chance encounter confirms why I love field recording: While walking on a trail near Lovin' Ovens recording footstep sounds, some people I met a few days prior—who were in a band together named Stilts—approached me. We stopped beside the trail, exchanged pleasantries, and they offered an improvised, trailside tune. Inexplicably, we nodded to each other, and, as gently as the piece unfolded, we strolled together along the trail as they played, and I recorded. Maybe you, too, feel as if you're walking when you listen. Either way, what a serendipitous and delightful encounter in Rainbowlandia.

The Whattobringia Toagatheringensis is an extremely versatile, small plant found anywhere in meadows and trails edge. It blooms in late spring into early summer. It has small, circular leaves, which are usually light green. It also grows quite large flowers, which can be purple, yellow, and red. Their somewhat slippery leaves are used topically for minor aches and pains. Particularly odd, and which continues to perplex botanists and language specialists alike, is their ability to communicate through a small vocal chord located in the xylem layer and verbalized by a protruding orifice that develops at the center of one of its flower petals, which, when the moon is full, it voices poetic platitudes, such as "dreams are postcards from elsewhere and are not reliant on belief."

Anywho, outside of peak brimming moon hour, it mostly speaks in a resourceful PSA loop, listing essential items one ought to consider bringing to a gathering. For example, here's a looped excerpt, "Include a backpack, flashlight, water bowel, cup, bowl, spoon, pocket knife, small pillow, eco-friendly soap & sanitizer, rope or twine, sleeping bag & pad, hiking shoes, warm and cold gear (you never know), snacks, water filter, toothbrush & toothpaste, prescription medications, raingear, first aid kit, towel, toilet paper, extra socks (you'll be glad you did), tent or tarp, a hat, musical instrument, work gloves....as well as, if able, things for the common good like shovels, prybars, axe, duct tape, buckets, a rugged cart or hand truck dolly, big tarps, fruit & veggies, chocolate, and so on it continues all the livelong day while it blooms.

15. JOY - HOT POTATO

Art by Pot Hotato

Recorded at the 2010 Pennsylvania Annual Rainbow Gathering, held in the Allegheny National Forest near the town of Sheffield, and featured on the *Pennsylvania 2010* compilation

LISTEN: ♫ 15. Joy - Hot Potato [3:14] ♫

"Love is like sunshine on a cloudy day" —Rainbow Trail Soundbite

Several moments come to mind when reviewing some of my favorite recording sessions over the years, including this impromptu session that arose when I thought I was heading to my tent to sleep. In all, six smokin' tunes were recorded due to my trail diversion, which you can find on the *Pennsylvania 2010* and *S'more Leftovers (2008-2010)* compilations (performed by Clint, Hella Regenerate, Joy, and Noah).

As friends and I approached Granola Funk Theater on a trail that paralleled Queen's Creek late in the evening on July 1st, a Singer-Songwriter/Open Mic event was happening at the theater. I recorded there earlier in the night for about an hour before venturing to other camps and kitchens. We spent most of the night elsewhere, but our tents were near Granola Funk. As we passed by, we noticed that the "primary" event appeared to have ended, but there were still around a dozen or so people hanging near the stage. Amidst their midst, we discerned familiar faces hailing from Faerie Camp. Their voices resonated with melodious and infectious tunes, akin to a sun-kissed meadow adorned with a vibrant tapestry of wildflowers, capturing one's attention with graceful allure.

I lingered in wakefulness far beyond my initial anticipation, ensnared by the enduring sounds that unfolded—each passing moment graced us with an exquisite succession of songs.

At one point, Joy stepped to the forefront to play *Hot Potato*, a song of seemingly unrequited love and travel.

She's leaving me tomorrow
She's hoppin' on that train
She'd rather wake up cold and lonely
Then beside of me again

But on Saturday, I'll see her
At a party with my friends
And with Ricky on the fiddle
She'll be in my arms again

In Ricky's absence, I frequently interweave fiddle bows and deft strokes within the tapestry of my thoughts, even though the composition brims with decorative instrumentation as I perceive it. These auditory embellishments are simply the intricate

pathways along which the panache of my mind navigates.

Joy's infectious vocal inflection nudged everyone to join in. The absence of prearranged singalong cues meant that unless one was already acquainted with the song, everyone else merrily improvised backup vocals and spontaneous sound effects.

Hot Potato
Hot Potato
Hot Potato
Hot Potato
Hot Potato
Hot Potato
Hot Potato
Hot Potato

What a playful chorus! Hot Potato exemplifies life on the road. The gripping song has such gleeful singing that you will hear different bits that bring you a smile upon each repeated listen.

She had to go to Memphis
To see her brother at a show
He ain't never been her baby
I said Baby, I don't know

That's why I call you hot potato
The way I'm playing catch with you
When you come back down and see me
You're a hoppin' pepper too

When you're dancing on my table
You're a sight that's mighty fine
When you're dancing in my doorway
You make me want to lose my mind

[0:00-0:15] Fade into a catchy guitar lick + a ripping belch ("Good out")
[0:40] A second guitar trickles in, rounding out the string weavings
[1:24-1:31] Delectable woos and a giggly giggle, just because
[2:08-2:14] I like the "Hoppin pepper too" line and response
[2:25-2:52] Marvelous and playful scat singing spills into the final verse
[3:07-3:14] Fade out into "You make me want to lose my mind."

It starts to rain rainbow droplets of letters that splatter into words upon the forest's damp floor. The moss shapes them into phrases, such as, "Folk tradition reversed becomes noitidart klof."

Nearby, a ghost pipe unravels a manifesto from one of its translucent leaves containing a multitude of droplets...

~ A Red Herring Manifesto ~

Irrelevant and misleading information owe their incarceration to a tiny number of reprehensible acts, and that, were it not for these distracting acts of honesty and integrity, which are, to some degree, victims of their imagination, in that it induces them not to pay attention to ignorance, malice, and greed. But their profound indifference to the way in which we integrate them, and even to the various punishments meted out to them, allows us to suppose they derive a great deal of comfort and consolation from their imagination, that they enjoy their sound reasoning, rational considerations, logical deductions, and infinite methodology in constructing run-on sentences. But in dreams, my friends and comrades, a red herring appears full-spectrum and vibrant, flexible and lubricious, and accordingly, poem scribbles, scratches, and scribes:

Someday is the maybe that never comes
The clouds only further life's unknowns
So whenever you are filled with scorn
Know that you are loved when you mourn

Someday is the maybe that never receives
The vague gesture simply burrows beneath
So whenever you succumb to such a potion
Know that you are more than just a notion

Someday is the maybe that never succeeds
The idea only creates riddled fatigue
So whenever you climb a hopeless song
Know that you are here and do belong

16. MICHAEL – INNER REVOLUTION

Art by Sermin Vupreme

Recorded at the 2004 California Annual Rainbow Gathering, held in the Modoc National Forest near the town of Likely, and featured on the *California* 2004 compilation

LISTEN:♫ 16. Michael – Inner Revolution [6:02] ♫

"Today I plan to hoof and horn my way to Main Circle because the trail realigns my shovel's chakras." —Rainbow Trail Soundbite

Inner revolution
Only true solution
That I've found across this nation
Return to the hoop of creation

The concept of the Inner Revolution beckons individuals to undertake a profound introspection of their convictions, principles, and routines, pinpointing realms where their participation might be inadvertently reinforcing detrimental patterns and behaviors. By becoming more self-aware and taking responsibility for their own personal growth, individuals can begin to transform themselves from the inside out like tectonic plates, giving rise to mountains of purpose and valleys of wisdom. This inner transformation can take many forms, including developing greater compassion and empathy for others, letting go of limiting beliefs and fears, cultivating a deeper perspective, and learning to live in greater alignment with one's true values and purpose—a simple recipe, yet challenging to execute flawlessly, in my experience. Although it seems mistakes and missteps are integral threads within the fabric of the human narrative, we possess the capacity to hone the weaving within the strands of change.

An inner revolution is a tempest within the soul, a storm of self-discovery that sweeps away the debris of conformity, leaving behind the fertile soil of authenticity. It's the alchemical cauldron where doubts and fears are melted down, transmuted into the molten gold of presence. Just as a caterpillar undergoes metamorphosis to emerge as a butterfly, an inner revolution is the chrysalis in which we cocoon our old selves, letting the winds of introspection sculpt them into new and vibrant forms.

Pull back the veils of what we knew
We look back we see we grew
Waken to our own soul
Rise, realize you're already old
Finding the balance to challenge
Open the doors, asking
Us to come on in again
Rising, remembering

While hanging out at Popcorner on the night of July 3rd, besides popcorn, of course,

lovely song-sharing occurred around the campfire by an assortment of people, always in flux depending on who came and went—sometimes you'd hear a singer-songwriter, a noodling instrumental, a Rainbow chant, or a stoned improv.

I had been recording a few friends by the time Michael played *Inner Revolution*, near dawn on July 4th, shortly before silence would commence. A low action on the guitar created a fret buzz sound. Whether done intentionally, by shifts in humidity or as a defective or damaged instrument, it is hypnotic and not at all off-putting. Michael tinkered with the guitar's action but decided to play it as it was, integrating the buzz. It reminds me of the buzzing sound associated with the mbira, the instrument traditional to the Shona people of Zimbabwe. According to tradition, the buzzing sound is intended to silence the mind's chatter.

Michael's alluring voice tends to quiet whatever mental chatter may distract me. It's a winsome song, contemplative and revelatory. Michael's sultry voice lulls one to gaze inward:

Inner Revolution
Only true solution
That I've found across this nation
Return to the hoop of creation

Inner Revolution summons, for me, what it means to gather and the inner revolution that can transpire. Thoughts unwind and meander reflectively...

Sometimes, someone, usually local media, will ask, "Aren't you escaping the world by going into the woods to pray for peace?" For me, that question disregards the healing power of nature, and the boost in mental health that being part of a community exerts, however temporary the experience may be. Long-term bonds and friendships have been cultivated as a result of Rainbow gatherings. Also, I quite like *escaping* the world from time to time in a book, playing or listening to music, producing or listening to radio shows/podcasts, gardening, going for a hike, you name it.

Modern society, gripped by capitalism, fosters isolation, and consequent poor mental health. Being a recusant against the forces that keep us all cloistered is a motivating factor to gather[6]. Although imperfect, every gathering provides immersion in nature, the opportunity to breathe in all that forest goodness, a template for catharsis, and

---

[6] Unless of course there's a pandemic...then, well, consider the health of yourself AND others too.

engagement in community-driven projects, such as digging shitters (slit trench latrines), hauling in supplies, laying water lines, and preparing meals. Moreover, money isn't a motivating factor in participating in said labor. Additionally, creative endeavors such as workshops and music provide a template for someone to recharge and heal their spirit. Or not. Another view might consider a gathering a frivolous endeavor filled with unsavory individuals, or simply one may prefer a more solo outdoor excursion. Hence, a gathering doesn't work for everyone all of the time (or anytime).

Nonetheless, the community spirit that creates a gathering remains a crucial reminder to recognize the inherent value of what can be achieved together.

Born in 1820, Florence Nightingale was an English social reformer and statistician who lived to be 90 years old, passing away in 1910. She is widely recognized as the founder of modern nursing. In her book, *Notes on Nursing: What It Is, and What It Is Not*, published in 1859, Nightingale discussed the relationship between the mind and body in terms of health, the positive impact of compassion and beauty on healing, and the soothing effects of nature. I mention this not only to highlight her incredible accomplishments but also because her insights remain relevant today, particularly in our screen-dominated world. Apply this to Rainbow, and the healing that a gathering provides for some becomes apparent. The Inner Revolution is in motion and never ends—Nothing Is Unachievable! Forge a New Path! Time for Change!

Ever so faintly during the song, you can hear birds chirping, signaling dawn's approaching light. After Michael finished playing, we gathered our belongings and returned to our camp to rest for a few hours before the noon Prayer for Peace. A soulful, accordant nightcap to color our body and mind, hopes and dreams, here in the hoop of creation.

Forgiveness for all the pain
Rising up again
I refuse to hold on anymore
To all those things making me tired and sore
Trying to find a way to overstand
So I can forgive you and let go again
Living in this moment or the one we've ever got
Got to remember who we are and not what we're not
The soul light shine like a butterfly

From a chrysalis soon we all shall fly
Soul remember when I see
Reflection of me
Your eyes evermore
Open the door

Notable Sonic Textures of Textured Sonic Notables:

[0:00-0:33] Fade into bird chirps and boots made for walkin', and that's just what they do; meanwhile, a gentle fingerpick tune slowly unfurls
[1:48] Well-timed campfire snap when Michael sings the word, "free"
[3:20-3:30] The whispery singing here gets me every time
[4:23-4:25] When Michael sings "Open the door" it feels like one does
[5:20-5:36] A tender fingerpick outro
[5:37-6:02] Fades out into bird chirps and more boots made for walkin', and that's just what they do; meanwhile, we hear a "We love You!"

You're somewhere whence you don't know exactly where yet, but who cares anyway, for the grove of white pines surrounding you sway and send you an air hug. The clouds twirl like a ballerina, the earth strums a fertile chord, and Maxim Maxi somersaults towards you and hands you a paper fortune teller. You play along—moving and shifting right and left, forward and back— soon revealing a hidden message, which states:

*** An ol' adage contends: the more you mix into it, the more you mix out of it ***

Trail wandering you go, oscillating slightly above and through the ground. A mosquito wearing a bowtie buzzes by and declares, "Carpe, veni, vidi, vici, diem."

The lichen beside you announces, "The jeans mustify the end."

Beside a woodpile sawing logs with words, Beaver Bill stops momentarily and shares a tongue-twister, "Repeat this five times fast: I saw some sawyers saw a saw with straw."

Somewhere hidden and sequestered with furtive pursuits, Shifty Saltlick, fiddling with fiddlesticks, alleges, "Shadow Council counseled before Shadow Counsel could council, thereby nullifying any of the councilors counsel conclusions."

Meanwhile, over yonder at the Seap What You Row Workshop, Wesourceful Wolf & The Wolf Packs have some basic howling packing pointers for building a relatively functional kitchen in the woods: food-grade and non-food-grade 5-gallon buckets (with lids), 15, 30, or 55-gallon food grade barrels for water storage, bleach, large pots & woks & grates & griddles & knives & bowls & spatulas & spoons & ladles, biodegradable dish soap & assorted scrubbies (for all your scrubbin' needs), spray bottles and misters, cutting boards, building tools, plenty o' tarps & cord, first aid kit, duct tape, propane burners and stoves (in case of a fire ban), bulk food, rugged and trail tested carts, lime for shitters, lighters, dishwashing tubs and/or buckets (never enough buckets), LED lights, trash bags, toilet paper, foot pump handwash components, water filters & water line, supply tent, and all the other things not mentioned here, until death do us part, Forever and Always, Amen.

16.9 SHILOH CIRCLE – CREAM ON ME

Art by Twark 'Sellow-bellied Wapsucker' Main

***** *Sound-Trail Diversion 9.0* *****

Recorded at the 2013 Montana Annual Rainbow Gathering, held in the Beaverhead National Forest near the town of Jackson, and featured on the *Montana 2013* compilation

LISTEN:♫16.9 Shiloh Circle – Cream On Me [2:07] ♫

"Every little bell in my bawdy is snappy" —Rainbow Trail Soundbite

Lean On Me is a soulful and uplifting song written and recorded by American singer-songwriter Bill Withers in 1972. The song was a massive hit. Over the years, I've heard and recorded several Rainbowfied "Weird Al" Yankovic-inspired remixes of popular songs, and Shiloh Circle's raunchy *Cream On Me* is a worthy addition to the bawdy song tradition and ranks among my mashup-up mondegreen favorites. Most people's familiarity with the original invited an immediate boisterous singalong accompaniment:

Sometimes in our life
We all get hard
We all get boners
But if we are wise
We'll unzip the flies
Of gay stoners

Cream on me after this song
And I'll be your friend
I'll help you fill the bong
For it won't be long
Till I'm gonna need
Somebody to cream on

The swashbucklers Kinky Lear & Flashy Falstaff follow up that creamtastic tune with another euphemistic, infectious, and scrumptious anthem, We Art Opening Up

We art opening up in sweet surrend'r
To the luminous loveth lighteth of the one (2x)
We art opening. We art opening. We art opening. We art opening.

We art rising up liketh a phoenix from the fireth;
Broth'rs and sist'rs—siblings—did spread thy wings and flyeth high'r (2x)
We art rising up. We art rising up. We art rising up. We art rising up.

We art opening up liketh a lotus floweth'r;
Alloweth the loveth lighteth shineth in our hearts tonight (2x)
We art opening. We art opening. We art opening. We art opening.

17. (A) POSSIBILITY – STARLING + (B) JEROME – CYCLES

Art by Bilba Bigleaf

Starling was recorded at the 2006 Colorado Annual Rainbow Gathering, held in the Routt National Forest near the town of Clark, and featured on the *Leftovers 2000-2008* compilation. *Cycles* was recorded at the 2011 Washinton Annual Rainbow Gathering, held in the Gifford Pinochet National Forest near the town Cougar, and featured on the *Washington* 2011 compilation

LISTEN: ♫17. (A) Possibility – Starling [1:03] + (B) Jerome – Cycles [1:51]♫

"My mossy cart hauls invisible liquid rakes frolicking air particulars in trail-land"
—Rainbow Trail Soundbite

Outlaw poetry, also known as outsider poetry or underground poetry, is a term used to describe a subversive and non-conformist approach to writing and performing poetry. It emerged as a movement in the mid-20th century and has continued to evolve and thrive through the decades.

The roots of outlaw poetry can be traced back to the Beat Generation of the 1950s and 1960s. Their work often tackled taboo subjects, explored personal and political themes, and experimented with form and language. The Beats challenged the traditional notions of poetry and sought to create a more raw, honest, and spontaneous form of expression.

The outlaw poetry movement gained further momentum in the 1960s and 1970s as various social and political movements were taking place, such as the civil rights movement, anti-war protests, and the feminist movement. They rejected mainstream poetry's academic and elitist tendencies, choosing instead to engage with the struggles of everyday people and marginalized communities. This performative aspect of outlaw poetry helped bridge the gap between poetry and other art forms, such as music and spoken word.

Recorded at an Open Mic/Spoken Word event hosted by Popcorner and MCed by Diamond Dave, *Starling* by Possibility is reminiscent of the outlaw poetry tradition. With evocative imagery and cogent metaphors, the spirit of the smokin' word sparks bonfires in zones mentally impoverished...

The rhyme is overflowing like the wine at Shabbat goblets
So rub your eyes and pockets with the tonic droplets

You tried to drop a spaceship on a comet but you lost it
You man-made mechanism they could not unlock it

Some turned to stone and nailed to crosses for trying to talk it
Surving harder relying on the harvest of the market

It's obvious the tribes are spread out like giant carpets
And this life is temporary, like subletting apartments
Eating with chopsticks living life in meager monetary margins
Sanctioned from celebration has got our people starving

Evolving will solve immeasurable problems
And clans of hobgoblins got nothing but plans
To dominate the whole entire micro and macrocosms

I dip into the rhythm like ladling soup out of cauldrons
Fallen forgotten ways shapeshifts and us evolvin'

To all my fellow earth-dwelling entities we are sovereign
A distant drum urgency eternities curtains parting

Embarking on epic journeys from day to when it's darkened
And sparkin' bonfires in zones mentally impoverished

We now shift our attention to visionary poetry, which colors *Cycles*, as told by friend, mentor, and visionary Jerome McGeorge. I have vivid memories of staying up late in the evening, waxing poetic and philosophical with Jerome. He's a visionary in the truest sense of the word. On top of that, he is an incredibly kind, caring, and compassionate human.

Recorded at an Open Mic/Spoken Word event at Popcorner/What Have You, again MCed by Diamond Dave, with Kristen Blinne. It was well-attended. Warm and fuzzy vibes surrounded the scene, and people listened quietly and intently. The campfire flickered with loud crackles, which underscored the auralscape. Chai and popcorn were served and—based on the yummy expressions—well received. The songs, stories, and poems were eclectic and varied, from young to old alike.

Visionary poetry is a genre of poetry that aims to convey deep insights, profound experiences, and spiritual or mystical visions. It often explores themes related to metaphysics, transcendence, and the human experience beyond the physical realm. Visionary poetry can be highly imaginative and employ rich symbolism and vivid imagery to evoke a sense of awe, wonder, and introspection.

Historically, visionary poetry has been present in various cultures, dating all the way back to the earliest records of writing. From the Odyssey to the Vedas, visionary poetry has left its stamp of wonderment. Other examples include the mystical poetry of Sufi poets like Rumi, the transcendental poetry of American poet Walt Whitman, the nature-themed poems of Mary Oliver, and the mystical works of William Blake, among others. These poets sought to go beyond the ordinary perception of reality and tap into higher states of consciousness, often using language that transcends traditional boundaries and conventions, celebrating the power of imagination, intuition, and spiritual exploration. It seeks to transcend the limitations of the ordinary world and invite readers to embark on a journey of self-discovery and enlightenment through the beauty and power of language. In *Cycles,* we again weave through evocative imagery:

> *In ages gone by*
> *Coiled within times to come*
> *Just after midnight*
> *Dragon bites her tail*

The opening passages verve morsels of insight, keen to see where the vision leads:

> *Art in our lives*
> *Because life is our art*
> *Members one of another*
> *Yet each do our part*

> *Future, androgynous, cooperative, and kind*
> *Millions the visionaries embrace creative mind*
> *The future we trust will be perfectly timed*

To (the) Moon It May Discern,

Sign me up for a future like that.

Signed, Let's Do This.

One Flew Over The Sound-Notes (Possibility):

[0:00-0:05] Fade into spoken-word piece title, "Starling"
[0:14-0:15] Quite the campfire's fiery snap that punctuates the words "Unlock it"
[0:25-0:33] Great sequence between the spoken word and the campfire
[0:57-1:03] Fade out into "And sparkin' bonfires..."

Two Flew Over The Noted-Sounds (Cycles):

[0:00-0:05] "In ages gone by..." (someone whispers: can I sit here?)
[0:28-0:33] "...in old must certainly fail." (the tail end of the phrase embellished with someone saying: "Put it down."). . . *yes, yes we will...*
[0:34-0:52] "Darkness lifers, pole shifts..." The distant drum circle seems to become more audible
[0:48-0:53] I like the random staccato singing that emerges in the foreground
[0:59-1:05] Impeccable timing for fire crackle with the line: "Creation! Fire! Burn at us all, be this light."
[1:03-1:15] The fire crackle appears stronger than before (or seems to anyway, in a RAW "what the thinker thinks, the prover proves" kind of way)
[1:47-1:51] Fade out into snap, crackle, and pop

A kind, sagacious spirit named Revenant Ritisha, who has seen much and experienced many worlds otherwise unseen by the unsuspecting lookie-loos, reads a poem at the Everlasting Bliss of Intergalactic Wordsmith Spoken Word & Open Mic event at the Campfire in the Sky.

~ The Mysterious Oscaria Zoroasternal ~

< < < O > > >

The wizard leads a shrouded life,
They mask the misery and the strife
They cast wide enigmatic dreams,—
Tossing as many names as schemes

But nothing is told of their life,
Do they have hardship, loss, or strife?
Mayhap we ask as a means of hope,—
With questions that widen our scope

To pierce the veil is our prayer,
Behind that another layer
Illusions of mischief at reign,—
A roving circus their domain

So while we sip from riddled rhymes
Our hearts and minds like seeds and vines
We to sleep and then we to wake,—
To move and flow and twist and shake

And when my gravestone kisses me
I'll glean from life's uncertainty
For vespers are curtains until,—
Imagination dips her quill

17.71 TOOL LOOT

Art by Rutrum Murtur

~ O ~

Tools come to rollick
Forging worlds with sturdy hands
Artisans of chance

18. BONOBOHOBO'S THREE-RING FREAK SHOW – LOVIN' YOU

Art by Kyndup Wee

Recorded at the 2012 Tennesse Annual Rainbow Gathering, held in the Cherokee National Forest near the town of Bluff City, and featured on the *Tennesse 2012* compilation

LISTEN:♫ 18. Bonobohobo's Three-Ring Freak Show – Lovin' You [5:30] ♫

"Lovin' you" —Rainbow Trail Soundbite

Lovin' You[7] is a classic love song recorded by Minnie Riperton in 1974. The song was written by Riperton and her husband, Richard Rudolph, and was produced by Stevie Wonder. Riperton initially developed the song's melody as a lullaby for her daughter, Maya Rudolph.

Bonobohobo's Three-Ring Freak Show performed a weird and eclectic set, including burlesque and double-entendre songs, as well as this oddly stunning cover of *Lovin' You* at the July 4th Variety Show at Granola Funk Theatre. The performer, adorned in a tin-draped and freaky face-painted clown character getup with a wind-up key attached to their back, sat before an equally tin-decorated toy piano. They looked like an enlarged music box. Since they were not named, let's call them Tinker Box for short-hand sake. The whole scene was a DMT-y cosmic visual to behold, particularly considering the backdrop.

That year, Granola Funk constructed a Pyramid stage wrapped in white fabric (a nod to the whole bugaboo surrounding the 2012 Mayan prophecy phenomenon). The bonus feature was the spaceship that soared by on a zipline, occasionally delivering popcorn to the audience below, thanks to Popcorner Camp poppin' away and refillin' the vessel as needed. It was a thing.

While Bonohobo performed, the white fabric backdrop made for sultry shadow puppetry during performances. It often got scrumptious, to say the least. With shadow dancers miming behind, the Three-Ring Freak peeps wound Tinker Box around and around. Before long, like a Golem made out of tin rather than clay, the inanimate became animate and moaned and struck the oddest version of *Lovin' You* that I've ever encountered.

Initially, it's so strange sounding, yet there's a seduction in the extravagant theatrics, like the way Tinker Box's commanding gaze entranced the audience, but behind the charm, there's a profoundly genre-bending allure in their legato, staccato, and vibrato-y vocal gymnastics. Almost like they are discovering a new way to look at melody and composition, inventing a new style of prosody.

The surrounding insect reverberations ooze another layer onto an already uncanny visual and soundscape.

Perhaps Tinker Box's approach to music is as alien as the spaceship that zoomed overhead midway through the performance.

Tinker Box jittered as they tinkered like they were devoid of lubrication. They played like any steampunk gear contraption made animate should, especially one dressed like a

---

[7] On a related note, it is common to hear someone say, "lovin' you" used as parting words between gatherers

clown. There was a groovy slow-motion dance between note strikings. At [3:27], the lack of lubrication and woundedness caused our animated performer to plop onto the piano, left as lifeless as the Grim Reaper's scythe.

But, of course, many were smitten with Tinker Box and yearned–*urged!*–for more, so Three-Ring Freak peeps obliged and wound them up again.

The insects continued to pulse, and Tinker Box finished with sultry sensations of beauteous song vibrations and then got up and pranced away like a fluid ballroom dancer.

I always wondered what it would be like if a toy music box came to life. And so it was. Tinker Box sounds exactly how I never expected one would, precisely how weirdness works.

Lovin' you is easy cause you're beautiful
Makin' love with you is all I wanna do
Lovin' you is more than just a dream come true
And everything that I do is out of lovin' you
La la la la la la la… do do do do do

The Adventures of Huckleberry Audio Timestamps:

[0:00-0:30] Fade into laughter, tinkling toy piano, and rhythmic insects
[0:42-0:46] Captivated by the Siren's song: "Yeeeeaaahhh"
[0:53-1:01] The most adorable tremolo vocal entry imaginable
[1:33-1:42] The "la la las" and insects merge
[2:25-3:00] You get the sense that the audience is wholly transfixed and enamored by the Music Box entity
[3:16-3:26] Music Box entity loses steam at "Springtiiiimmme"; winders wanted at Gfunk
[3:33-3:44] "Should we wind her up again?" - - - "YES! WIND HER UP!!"
[3:45-3:55] Drum kit kicks a lick while a stagehand says, "Let's count, huh: 1–2–3–69!!"
[3:59-4:14] Music Box entity reboots. There is much laughter
[5:00-5:06] My oh my: "And every time that we yooooooooouuuuuuuuuuu"
[5:15-5:30] Fade out into "la la las" and screams and applause and laughter

Afterward, Tinker Box ponders as they walk backstage:

"I used to think I was a human dreaming I was a bot, but now I am not sure if I am a bot dreaming I am human."

POOF! Like Faierie dust, you whisk away down a checkered-flagged trail.

18.1 CHAVAN – SONG FOR THE MOON

Art by Fluffy-backed Wit-babbler

***** *Sound-Trail Diversion 10.0* *****

Recorded at the 2008 Wyoming Annual Rainbow Gathering, held in the Bridger-Teton National Forest near the town of Pinedale, and featured on the *Wyoming 2008* compilation

LISTEN:♫ 18.1 Chavan – Song For The Moon [1:38] ♫

"They used a whisk to point the way to the Haulin Trash Workshop."
—*Rainbow Trail Soundbite*

The moon evokes beauty, mystery, and allure. Whether romantic, mysterious, or foreboding, she captivates poets, seekers, dreamers, and schemers alike. At the July 1st Open Mic Night at Granola Funk Theater, Chavan enchanted everyone with an unaccompanied, magical song:

Moon sister rising
Over the Sandia Mountains
Yellow like a dandelion
You are the queen of the night sky
You are the queen of the night sky
Creating magical nights
With your fairytale lights
Through the stars
And I'm feeling the craze
As I bask in your rays once again
And we howl at you
As we dance the night through
Just because
Just because
You are the light in the dark of night
You are the light in the dark of night

The Ittylus Bittyma is an uncommon, tiny plant, but hardy. It can be found in a variety of zones throughout the world, if you know where and when to look, in fields and forests similarly, often growing in tiny clusters. It has thin, triangle-shaped leaves, which are usually dark green. It also produces large flowers, which span all the colors of the rainbow, usually blooming from

spring through early summer, and rely on cross-pollination to reproduce. Its leaves are psychoactive and, when smoked, produce a powerfully hallucinogenic and mind-altering effect. Ritual use of the plant, according to Tiny Camp, dates back thousands of years. Users often report life-affirming impacts on their outlook on the relationship with life, death, and the interconnectedness of all beings. In 1972, the Tiny Camp community gained legal protection from the Universal Plant Spirits Congress (UPSC) to oversee domestic production, fulfill the growing global demand for medicinal use, and protect wild varieties from over-harvesting the plant. We have Tiny Camp to thank for their massive role in helping make a more well-adjusted global society thanks to the transformative and insightful powers of the wee and fair Ittylus Bittyma.

19. TESSA - IT COULD BE SO EASY

Art by Possum O'Possum

Recorded at the 2022 Colorado Annual Rainbow Gathering, held in the Medicine Bow-Routt National Forest near the town of Hayden, and featured on the *Colorado 2022* compilation

LISTEN:♫ 19. Tessa - It Could Be So Easy [3:41] ♫

"Paint me a stirfry and I'll read a blue tarp on the way to the spring of eternal twine. "
—Rainbow Trail Soundbite

Notice how, drawn together by an intrinsic, ethereal kinship that transcends boundaries, music does. This, indeed, of music is the wondrous accordance and revelation bestowed by the realm. Profoundly stirring, the experience is, for music unveils the undeniable truth that while we each bear a singular peculiarity of individuality lies a harmonizing beneath the veneer, a resonance that unites us. Yes, hmmm...

Going down these unseen roads
Feeling lost but not quite gone

The moon is in the waxing gibbous phase. It's July 4th at the Granola Funk Rainbow Variety Show, and the night comes alive with stars shining overhead. The air perfumes faint gusts of mystery from the aspen trees, with the smell of wild onion and the invisible greenness of what makes life worth living. There is a moment of almost silence, but a silence that breathes with the soft breathing of the trees and, in the acute sound of fresh mountain air, insistently, incessantly flows on the breath of its own deep aliveness. Far away, the passage of time chugs along like a long caress, moving ploddingly, with an inexorable determinedness, across the warm living bodyscape, whence from the land of timelessness, unfurls a most perfect song.

And I'll be your home
If we just do keep the lights on

It Could Be So Easy left a lasting, indelible impression on me. It was my favorite song I heard (and in turn recorded) at that gathering. I always feel an Autonomous Sensory Meridian Response (ASMR) tingling sensation whenever I listen to it—a herald song showcasing the healing power of music.

When push comes to shove
Be the first one to love

Tessa channeled beauty in song. One could feel ripples of beauty wave throughout everyone who sat and listened. It was a soul-stirring performance, resonated by her graceful and soothing melody and yearnful—call to action—lyrics that passionately beckon for love to

guide the way~

It could be so easy
Livin' life like this

What Audio Dreamscapes May Come:

[0:00-0:05] Fade into a strumming spell
[0:50-0:55] Arbitrary timestamp note to say how much I love how the barely audible distant drum circle gives the song a deeply soothing undercurrent that is as cuddly as a cat purr
[1:16-1:23] Melt my heart won't you
[2:00-2:01] "YEAH!"
[2:25-2:28] "Something, something coffee....shhhh"
[2:38-2:42] Melt my heart won't you, again
[3:07-3:17] Spring-tingles every time
[3:30-3:41] Fade out into a melodious send-off. Someone punctuates an exclamation point, "I would buy your album!"

You don't question why you're tightrope walking with others on an invisible paracord between the moon's crescent points. Dreams hold lunar infusions in high regard, so perhaps the logic is sound. Besides, the folk around here lore about night wandering exaltations upon the trail of singing together.

You suddenly find yourself descending upon a slippery slope, which, your friend Ostentatious Owl reminds you (i.e., owlsplains), is a logical fallacy that erroneously makes assumptions about a sequence of occurrences that could culminate in a significant incident, frequently an unfavorable one, without providing countering evidence that this will transpire. Thus, con cuidado, take care, have care. *The path ahead is as slippery as logic itself. All the more dream-trail reason one needs to gift wrap poetic messages from otherness:*

~ 12 Days of Presence ~

On the first day of presence
A true thought sent to me:
A Druid in a Deep See

On the second day of presence
A true thought sent to me:
Two Magic Wands
And a Druid in a Deep See

On the third day of presence
A true thought sent to me:
Three Hands Bent
Two Magic Wands
And a Druid in a Deep See

On the fourth day of presence
A true thought sent to me:
Four Falling Words
Three Hands Bent
Two Magic Wands
And a Druid in a Deep See

On the fifth day of presence
A true thought sent to me:
Five Might Dings
Four Falling Words
Three Hands Bent
Two Magic Wands
And a Druid in a Deep See

On the sixth day of presence
A true thought sent to me:
Six Bells a Playing
Five Might Dings
Four Falling Words
Three Hands Bent
Two Magic Wands
And a Druid in a Deep See

On the seventh day of presence
A true thought sent to me:
Seven Songs a Singing
Six Bells a Playing
Five Might Dings
Four Falling Words
Three Hands Bent
Two Magic Wands
And a Druid in a Deep See

On the eighth day of presence
A true thought sent to me:
Eight Sirens a Musing
Seven Songs a Singing
Six Bells a Playing
Five Might Dings
Four Falling Words
Three Hands Bent
Two Magic Wands
And a Druid in a Deep See

On the ninth day of presence
A true thought sent to me:
Nine Sages Sighing
Eight Sirens a Musing

Seven Songs a Singing
Six Bells a Playing
Five Might Dings
Four Falling Words
Three Hands Bent
Two Magic Wands
And a Druid in a Deep See

On the tenth day of presence
A true thought sent to me:
Ten Ogres a Rowing
Nine Sages Sighing
Eight Sirens a Musing
Seven Songs a Singing
Six Bells a Playing
Five Might Dings
Four Falling Words
Three Hands Bent
Two Magic Wands
And a Druid in a Deep See

On the eleventh day of presence
A true thought sent to me:
Eleven People Plotting
Ten Ogres a Rowing
Nine Sages Sighing
Eight Sirens a Musing
Seven Songs a Singing
Six Bells a Playing
Five Might Dings
Four Falling Words
Three Hands Bent
Two Magic Wands
And a Druid in a Deep See

On the twelfth day of presence
A true thought sent to me:
Twelve Seekers Striving
Eleven People Plotting
Ten Ogres a Rowing
Nine Sages Sighing
Eight Sirens a Musing
Seven Songs a Singing
Six Bells a Playing
Five Might Dings
Four Falling Words
Three Hands Bent
Two Magic Wands
And a Druid in a Deep See

152

20. HUMAN - SIMPLE WAYS

Art by Sunsign Moontwine

Recorded at the 2009 New Mexico Annual Rainbow Gathering, held in the Santa Fe National Forest near the town of Cuba, and featured on the *New Mexico 2009* compilation

LISTEN: ♫ 20. Human - Simple Ways [5:35] ♫

"Look for the signs in the signs that are everywhere within the counsel's ladle scoops"
—Rainbow Trail Soundbite

Reclining within a meadow, beneath a canopy of twinkling stars, enveloped by the ethereal choreography of fireflies' luminous waltz, the distant, melodious whippoorwill's evening serenade emerging from the adjacent woods evokes the enchantments of a simple life...

Recorded sometime in late June at Funkapoo Knoll—a neighborhood comprised of Popcorner Camp, an unnamed small coffee/tea hut, and Funkapoo Kitchen. The three camps utilized one campfire for evening revelry and ember gazing. Human and friends stopped by to play a set of music. Human played guitar and lead vocal, Brockell played fiddle and backup vocal, and others occasionally joined in on banjo, percussion, guitar, and singing.

Human, a talented songwriter, played many timeless golden greats that night. *Simple Ways* is a quintessential bucolic embrace of rural living. The song begins with cheerful campfire chatter. A guitar and fiddle soon invite us to wander down a country road. The campfire crackles rhythmic undertones, making a cozy song even cozier.

I met Human in 2006 when he played a show at a cafe in Madison, Wisconsin. Several of us went skinny dipping in Lake Mendota following the show. It was great, splashy fun. He has always been kind and gracious about having campfire field recording sessions. In all, there are around 20 recordings from various gatherings over the years.

Simple Ways, a gorgeous tune, reminds me of the type of songs brewed out of the Americana folk tradition in the 1970s by the likes of Emmylou Harris, Gram Parsons, and John Prine. The popcorn and the chai were served a-plenty, smiles & laughter were shared in abundance, and a timeless recording session transpired. Brockell adds delicious fiddle strokes and soothing backup vocals. Humans' country folk delivery is as warm as a handmade quilt. The New Mexico gathering was especially memorable. A vibrant double rainbow appeared shortly after the Prayer for Peace at High Noon on July 4th. A sense of wonderment and elation swept over many, ushering in a tide of jubilant celebrations, almost as if the presence of the double rainbow itself bestowed a benediction. Indeed, my heart holds an ardent affection for such unadorned and genuine expressions of joy. Oh, how I love those simple ways~

Some people like the tv
Not me I just watch the sky
Felt a better sense of freedom
Watching the hawks and eagles fly

In the sound of the rivers
Running free out to the sea
Running through the canyons
Yeah, that's what fills me

It's time to plant our gardens
Get ready for another year
Take advantage of this weather
While the sky's still blue and clear

Corn and beans, squash and kale
Like to grow together
Save our seeds and keep them dry
And we'll be eating right forever

Give me a simple life in the country
Where I can be free
Give me a fresh spring and a garden
It's all that I need
I need an Earth home on this planet
To live out my days
My heart really loves those simple ways

Nice stretch in the morning
Rise and say hi to the sun
Know we got a lot of work to do
And there's enough for everyone

Rains gonna be coming soon
We got a lot of wood to move
We gotta keep this family dry
If it's the only thing we do

Give me a simple life in the country

Where I can be free
Give me a fresh spring and a garden
It's all that I need
I need an earth home on this planet
To live out my days
My heart really loves those simple ways

Real food from the garden every day
Jar enough if we don't eat it
Putting it away
Life is our own village
Listen to the children play
Swim in the river at the end of the day

Give me a simple life in the country
Where I can be free
Give me a fresh spring and a garden
It's all that I need
I need an Earth home on this planet
To live out my days
My heart really loves those simple ways
My heart really loves those simple ways
My heart really loves those simple ways

Additional Sounds Within Times of Sound Within Sounds Additional Times of Sound:

[0:00-0:13] Fade into a guitar opening riff and people shouting out what they're going to do to make the world a better place. One kid says, "Make a machine that converts cow farts into fresh air."
[0:14-0:15] "Dumpy!"
[0:18-0:42] The fiddle eases in bow by bow

[1:33-1:57] Beautiful chorus singing
[2:25-2:45] The wood we used had a high resonance that sounded at times like sparklers
[3:42-4:13] Nice build into some spaciously smooth fiddle flourishes
[4:38-5:13] Lovely singing through and through—hoots, howls, and all
[5:14-5:35] Fade out into simple ways

Nebulous Newt, has silky, soft, and fair skin, often moist, which delightfully compliments its cheekbones. Their brilliant ember-like bioluminescence eyes, set narrowly on top of their noggin', placed comfortably in their body, sit beside a spring between fallen leaves, observes discreetly at the humans squabbling, bickering, fussing, and a-fightin' over silly little things. There's something appealing about Nebulous Newt, perhaps it's their sense of humor, or maybe it's simply their eerie insight into unpacking the human condition better than humans are even capable of examining given the conditions. Ergo, they penned a country duet. It goes like this [insert your favorite folky chord sequence]

~ Darling Lonesome Mirror ~

~o~

Darling Lonesome, what is it that you see?
For your eyes are not spies in the mirror
Upon your gaze blinks your only clue
And therein lies the truths you already knew

Seeker:
Mirror, Mirror on the wall
Who's the fairest of them all?
Humankind said they'd heed the call,
But their absence looms come nightfall

Magic Mirror:
Seeker, Seeker on the floor
Have I not shown you the door?
You are blind by ancient lore
A heart stuck surely won't soar

Darling Lonesome, what is it that you bring?
For objects are trifle things for the queen
Beneath your stare, unhand what you grip,
And therein lies the truths you let slip

Seeker:
Mirror, Mirror on the wall
Who's the fairest of them all?
Humankind said they'd heed the call,
But their absence looms come nightfall

Magic Mirror:
Seeker, Seeker on the floor

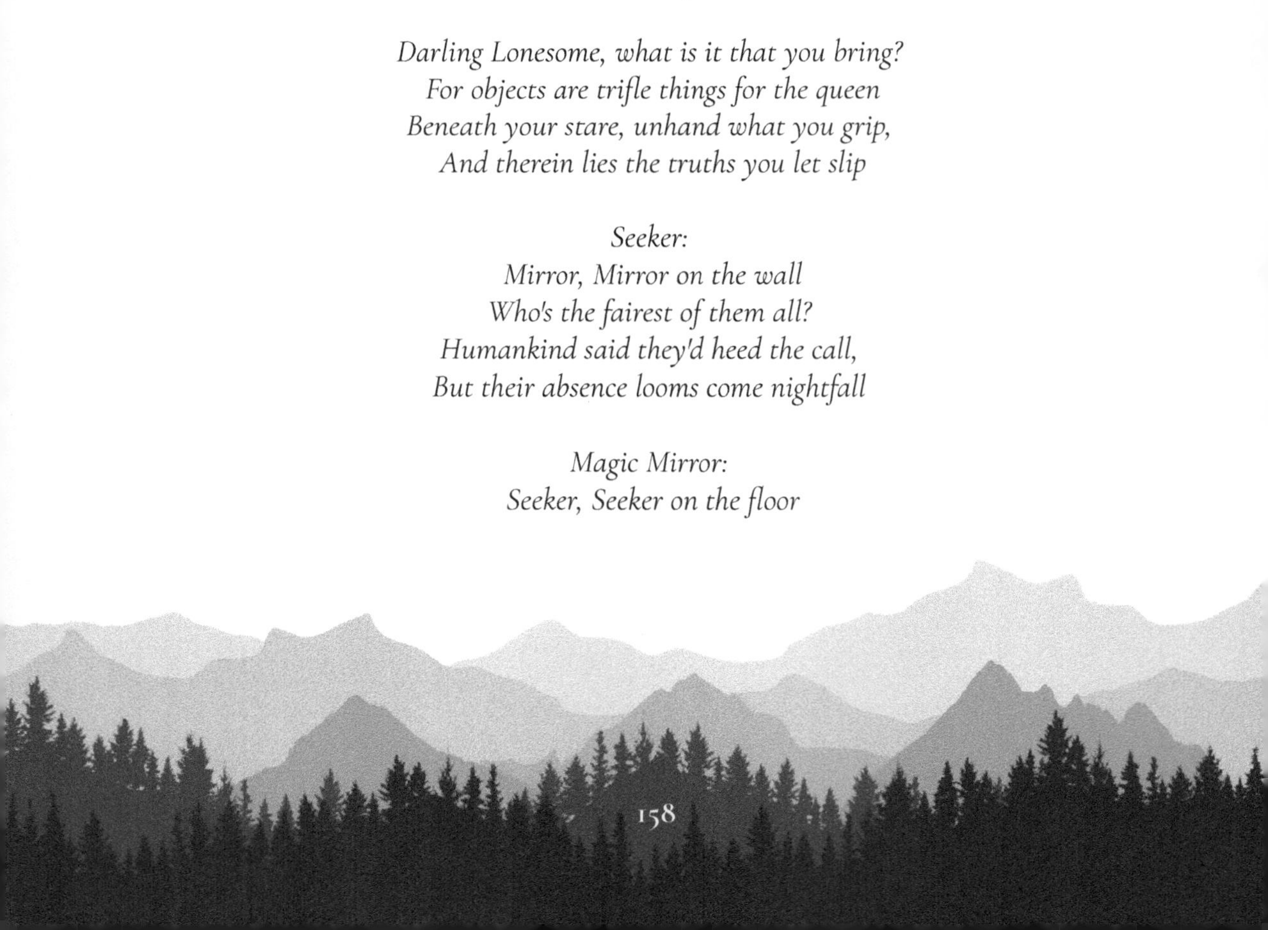

Have I not shown you the door?
You are blind by ancient lore
A heart stuck surely won't soar

160

20.3 THE TEAFAERIE – MAPPING THE SOURCE

Art by The Shimmering Elf Society

***** *Sound-Trail Diversion 11.0* *****

Recorded at the 2017 Oregon Rainbow Gathering, held in the Malheur National Forest near the town of John Day, and featured on the *Oregon 2017* compilation

LISTEN:♫ 20.3 The Teafaerie – Mapping the Source [11:25] ♫

"Love is flowing" —*Rainbow Trail Soundbite*

It was late afternoon on July 3rd when Teafaerie and I wandered to a quiet place away from the main encampment area to record her epic poem, *Mapping the Source*[8]. We found a pretty meadow area and used a fallen log as a table to prop up the small tripod I occasionally use for my microphone. You could see a few other people in the distance; otherwise, it was just us. Quietness pervaded, save for birdsong and the occasional barely audible distant yelps and whatnot from gatherers. Imagine mashing up Lewis Carroll by adding a heap of Speculative Fiction, a scoop of mind-wandering fantasy, a handful of mindful trip guidance, and a dollop of visionary insight and wisdom. Line by line, it's genuinely an astonishing poem. Sit back, listen contemplatively, and muse away. It begins as follows:

Mapping the source! What a marvelous jest!
The Trickster's mischievous meddling has blessed
psychedelic cartography's quixotic quest
with an answer whose question cannot be expressed.

The Center is everywhere, you are the light.
An internal eternity, empty and bright,
where opposites merge, and all versions unite.
Enter into the infinite. Do it tonight!

The stars flicker sparkles that transform into an iridescent waving banner that reads: "May the moon shine where elegance strides." Fluttering in front of you, Julietea Romeotime Flaps her

---

[8] Read the poem at Teafaerie's column on erowid.org, the information site on psychoactive plants, chemicals, and related issues. https://www.erowid.org/columns/teafaerie/2016/05/17/mapping-the-source/

wings into your slip-dream and sings a wave-watery verse-beam:

The riv'r is flowing (moth'r carryeth me)
The riv'r the lady is flowing
Fowing and growing
The riv'r the lady is flowing
Down (back) to the flote
Moth'r (moon shall) carryeth me
(H'r) issue I shall at each moment beest
Moth'r (moon shall) carryeth me
Down (back) to the flote

21. MJ – LOVE IS DIVINE

Art by Farout Happenwell

Recorded at the 2000 Montana Annual Rainbow Gathering, held in the Beaverhead National Forest near the town of Jackson, and featured on the *Montana 2000* compilation

LISTEN:♫ 21. MJ – Love Is Divine [5:41] ♫

"Love is divine, divine is love" —Rainbow Trail Soundbite

Divine Love is an essential element in many spiritual traditions and refers to the idea of a love that transcends human understanding and is beyond our limited human experience. Divine Love is often associated with the idea of god(dess) or the divine and is believed to be a force that connects all living beings and sustains the universe. If love is god(dess) and god(dess) is change, then divinity is constant.

MJ, on guitar and vocal, accompanied by a hotchpotch Gfunk House Band, performed his song, *Love is Divine,* a paean to the Divine. I remember this as one of the later performances that year at the July 4th Variety Show at Granola Funk Theater. It was probably, let's say, around 420 AM, and many were still hanging out and engaged. I'd call this performance a classic old-school Gfunk moment.

We begin with a slow guitar riff, upright bass thumps, a piping flute, and various sorts of percussion, including mouth slaps. MJ's verse imbues gratitude through descriptive imagery. The backing music builds tension by not rushing (it's the journey, not the destination, according to the well-trod adage). We get the sense we are slowly building to somewhere grand—and beautiful. Swirling harmonies respond in kind, punctuating the phrases with affectionate embellishments.

A seraphic chorus that immediately prompted many to sing along. At [4:20], it seems nearly everyone in attendance joins in, bewitched, and it truly becomes an ecstatic moment into the final notes and line—*your love is diiiiivvviiiiiinnnnnee.* O, how mellifluous~

> *You are the goddess*
> *Shining song of the ages*
> *And the sacred prayer of the sages*
> *And your light shines like a beacon from on high*
> *Light shining like a beacon*
>
> *So sacred and beautiful*
> *Mother for all time*
> *Sharing of love*
> *Eternal*

To unite with the ways divine
To unite with the ways divine
To unite with the ways divine
To unite with the ways divine

Your one love is divine
Your love is divine
Your one love is divine
Your love is divine
You're glowing more above in the sky
You're waxing and you're waning
Your cycle ever flowing and waving
And your smile shines like a giant light from the sky
Shining like the sun
Smile, reflecting the blessings of the sun
Smile
So sacred and beautiful
Mother for all time
Sharing of love
Eternal

To unite with the ways divine
To unite with the ways divine
To unite with the ways divine
To unite with the ways divine

Your one love is divine
Your love is divine
Your one love is divine

Your love is divine

<u>Note-Warming Timestamps of Sonic This:</u>

[0:00-0:06] Fade into a whispering flute and guitar riff
[0:07-0:10] Upright bass thumps from stage right
[0:40-1:10] Some kind of woodblock percussion that I never noticed or heard before until writing this aural timestamp
[1:18-1:45] Love the vocal weavings
[2:28-2:30] Well-played exquisite random vocal trill embellishment (and why I love field recording at Rainbow gatherings)
[3:20-3:42] Mellifluous flute playing
[3:50-4:20] Another mighty fine section of vocal weaving
[4:44-5:00] A call for "A cappella" flows right into just that, a cappella, which is glorious
[5:38-5:41] Fade out into love is divine

In a land near and dear not whithersoever, the forest was vast, shadowy, misty, and dense. Its canopy was eclipsed by unusually tall hawthorn, the protective shrub, complemented the vast stands of iconic maple and healing ash. Below sprawled passionate rhododendrons, which provided just enough openings for light to pass down for the dispersed magic ferns to blanket the roots, duff, and dirt. Curling singers dangled from many a tree, and a medley of various hued flowers clung to any space they could find, catching attention in the otherwise verdant scenery. A cacophony of alien sounds, predominantly those of insects conspiring in the terra firma, resonated through the air and formed a lush orchestra with the cascading sound ripples coming from a waterfall in the distance. Soon, from out of the past tense to the now tense unveils a melodious yet sobering chant that waves through the trees:

Mother Earth, guide us strong
Through our fears, move them along
We're here in spirit, we're here in song
Here for you as the years grow long

Hopeful Humming Hummingbird, who flutters in empathy and vulnerability, and optimism and courage too, glistens its wings of intention, flickering this dream-scene into a very real scene of climate change, mass extinctions, and injustices a-plenty, shares a very nectar-fueled call to action:

"Hear ye! Hear ye! Brethren and Sistren and Nonbinaryen! Take direct action if the moment calls to defend our Mother Earth. Verily, in solidarity and mutual aid, we'll have each other's back. We're all woven webs in Indra's net. Don't let them strip mine your wisdom nor clearcut your hope. Don't listen to the naysayers who say there isn't enough money because money's just duff anyway. The pursuit of power is a tiresome quest. But If drama didn't exist, we'd have to invent it, but I digress. May our doing say how the doing gets done! May our creativity flow like magic. May we transform the troubles-n-trials into a world that is more cooperative, caring, and kind. A warm smile goes a long way. The sunrise brings in a new day, perhaps even ushering in a terra firma new way. So buckle up your bootstraps, for we have work to do. Wash your hands. Don't touch your thing to the thing. Cover your shit. Safety first. Mother Earth is our home, but never forget that she bats last...Welcome Home."

21.12 BLEST SPRING IN THE SKY

Art by Grimm Frost & Earthicolor 'This Is Not A Map' Productions

You're in some kind of dream within a dream within a dream, you see some families sitting together, deeply engaged in a playground clapping rhyme:

Blest spring in the sky
Life's crucial ally
You float way up high
Without you, we die

172

21. MANDOLIN – VIOLIN FIDDLE VIOLIN FIDDLE DREAM

Art by Infinitea 'Woodchoppin'' Templespore

Recorded at Green Path at the 2010 Pennsylvania Annual Rainbow Gathering, held in the Allegheny National Forest near the town of Sheffield, and featured on the *Pennsylvania 2010* compilation

LISTEN:♫ 21. Mandolin – Violin Fiddle Violin Fiddle Dream [1:43] ♫

"The directions said to do the mambo, but I turned left instead and found myself at the Angel Cakewalk" —Rainbow Trail Soundbite

I don't always attend or record the July 1st Singer-Songwriter/Open Mic Night at Granola Funk Theater, but when I do, I do.

Before embarking on a nighttime stroll with friends to what was for us, an unexplored area of the gathering, we sat and listened to various performances. During that time, I recorded a beguiling performance by Mandolin, which I inexplicably entitled *Violin Fiddle Violin Fiddle Dream*. I customarily invent a placeholder title if the proper one is unknown or unable to track down later.

After being introduced by the MC, they hopped on stage, and, wasting little time, went right into playing this trance-inducing instrumental.

There were several hundred people in attendance by that point, and with minimal background chatter, we were engulfed in the bowed vibrations. The fiddle may draw some of the exterior noises out, but I imagine many listened intently, spellbound by Mandolin's performance.

At around [0:53], as the bow moves to a higher register, I often experience a soothing brain tickle similar to using a metal tine scalp massager. Throughout the piece, the bowed strokes entice me to follow the rabbit down the hole.

At Granola Funk, the quality of performances can be unpredictable, regardless of the night's theme. While some moments may be filled with glorious performances, there may also be long gaps of less interesting content. However, at 3 a.m., when you least expect it, you might be treated to the most gorgeous song you've ever heard. I touched on this marvel earlier (in *Sound-Trail 11. Danjhel – Cosas Bellas*). Someone is always awake at Rainbow, so essentially, magic has the potential to occur at any hour.

This instrumental is so nice I often hit replay and listen twice. When I need to let off some steam, this tune puts me into a dream.

These Aural Onomatopoeia Notes From Notes Onomatopoeia Aural These:

[0:00-0:04] Fade into a fiddler's dream
[1:13-1:19] Hilarious baby makes babbling vocalizations, sounds ancient, primordial, even
[1:39-1:43] Fade out of a fiddler's dream, maybe

While sitting beside a campfire, a gnome-like being waltzes beside you and banters, "As the birds sing, as the wind speaks, as the music is, so are the folk upon the trail."

Also sitting by the fire, a griffin, expectantly bull guards a joint, yawns a proverb: "When gravity gets you down, choose to look up."

Meanwhile, situated a short distance away, a Banshee sits at the Spirit House and weepingly keens a farewell song. . . . . .

All of a sudden, you're swirling around the Main Boogie Pit & Heart Fire, rumbling in the mud of booming beats in a galloping all-in-one rhythm. Your head is in the clouds, and your body has gone—or better yet—gnome with it. Fluid and floaty in the galaxy of life's mysteries, painting words with a quill dipped in a pail of aurora borealis swirling with deep wonderin' and a-ponderin' & yearin' and a-churnin' collage of colors upon a canvas of dark matters even if dark matter unmatters when life gets lost in a black hole, you unfurl the following nursery rhyme meets metaphysics verse.

~ Questions Answers Mysteries Musings ~

May the valley of the unknowns
Lead us on a starry path
Where we may find ourselves
In the freckled glory of existence

< Who started it? >

There was a crooked thought,
And it went a crooked mile
It found a crooked wonder,
Against a crooked smile

It was a crooked life
Which wrote a crooked book,
And they all lived together,
With a curious crooked look

< Are we going to make it? >

The other evening, the sun was like a blood-red rose,
But it was of a kind unsniffed by a romantic nose
An ominous vestibule seeped the pains of the earth,
And upon the sky were splattered cries for one's rebirth

< Where are we going to put it? >

Humankind, put the essence on,
Humankind, put the essence on,
Humankind, put the essence on,
And let's have divinity

Living, so it goes again,
Living, so it goes again,
Living, so it goes again,
Death moves our way

< Who's going to clean it up? >

O Spirit forever with the changing vessel turns to foresee
How we laugh at ideas while our questions make swishes
Gentle as warm air, we venture among many a jubilee
This circling flow serves what comes down to the dishes

< Is it serious? >

Hinkey, dinkey, soda crackers,
Hinkey, dinkey, boo,
Hinkey, dinkey, soda crackers,
Out goes you,
Gaze in the moonlight and fear not the sight

Fillison, Follason, Nicholas Juan
Pluck on the lore-string to unleash a sprite
Stinkalum, Stankalum, Buck!

Bee, to be, a bumble bee
Stung a man on his knee
And a hog upon the snout
I'll be dogged if you ain't out

Teacups and wonders,
Plates and wishes,
All little minds
Wear calico britches
Out goes Y-O-U, sky blue!

Life is quick it's gone lickety-split
How scrumptious the moments of what we get
And don't you never ever, in any weather, forget
We, as one amoeba who chose to mix it up and split

We are what we are in the all that is all
And th-th-th-that's all, folks!

22.2 FAYE ADINDA- LET MY LIGHT SHINE THROUGH

Art by Boggy Britches

***** *Sound-Trail Diversion 12.0* *****

Recorded at the 2023 New Hampshire Annual Rainbow Gathering, held in the White Mountain National Forest near the town of Berlin, and featured on the *New Hampshire 2023* compilation

LISTEN: ♫ 22.2 Faye Adinda - Let My Light Shine Through [6:39] ♫

"We're over here until here becomes there or there becomes here." —Rainbow Trail Soundbite

Light, brilliant illumination, gleaming eternally, radiant brightness, the awakening of the soul, our guide through the darkness, where divinity shines upon itself, so eminence finds its way, leading us back home to each other...

Now, I could spend all of my time dreaming about the future
Or I could spend all of my time dwelling on my past
Or I could be here and breathe the love in this present moment
And do the best with what I have

I'm going to let my light shine through
I'm going to let my light shine through
I'm going to let my light shine through

Recorded at the Rainbow Family Variety Show on July 4th at Granola Funk Theater. Faye performed a few songs that night, all warmly received. This one, *Let My Light Shine Through,* makes me feel all warm and fuzzy—simply wonderful.

Regardless of the subject matter, I love old spirituals, for the energy of unity evoked transcends the limits of language and belief. The spirit of music and love emanates undiminished. Those old songs create connection, which is what's most important. And then sometimes you hear a new song that reinvigorates said spirit and spiritual song tradition. Faye's *Let My Light Shine Through* accomplishes this remarkably well, with lyrics emanating universal oneness through choosing light over darkness, glows with a heavenly melody. One of the most beautiful songs I heard at that gathering. New Hampshire was wet and rainy, yet we were tasked to let our light shine through.

We're undergoing a planetary crisis, and may we meet this moment by not letting that spark within go out. Nor shall we allow the spirit of apathy to reign supreme. Let's meet doom with preparedness. This little light of yours, let it shine, shine through the fear,

the hate, the othering of others, the lines drawn in the sand, borders. It is essential that we continue to keep the home fires burning, where we actively build an inclusive world of peace, love, compassion, and understanding—may the unfathomable lightness of being shine through~

You are suddenly as light as the aether, and you begin to levitate and drift from one campfire to another, observing a campfire within a campfire within a campfire, a circle within a circle, while dreaming about Rainbow, much like Rainbow dreams of itself. You catch a compelling soundbite as you float by along an unmarked trail:

> *"Everyone has a different dreamscape, and every dreamscape might tell*
> *us something interesting about our world, if we are willing to listen."*
> *— Roberta Antenna Willsun*

182

22.3 WIND CHIMES CHIMIN' I

Art by Mouse Ogre & The Projection Map Collective

***** *Sound-Trail Diversion 13.0* *****

Recorded at the 2019 Wisconsin Annual Rainbow Gathering, held in the Chequamegon–Nicolet National Forest near the town of Iron River, and featured on the *Wisconsin* 2019 compilation

LISTEN:♫ 22.3 Wind Chimes Chimin' I [1:48] ♫

"Folks are washing heartsongs at Nic@Nite while chanting down headlamps of burnt rice"
—Rainbow Trail Soundbite

En route to the gathering, I found some homemade wind chimes at a yard sale at a rural house on a back road in the Northwoods. The chimes were suspended using fishing line fastened to a rustically adorned ring crafted from lures. I hung it in a tree near Canthook Lake and hit record. The breeze took care of the rest...

In a future way backeth at which hour, a p'rson who is't claim'd those gents w're the real Shakespeare, although their claims, according to some, seemeth rath'r tenuous, didst a thing. Thence, they unveil'd a scroll madeth out of birch bark, did hop on the supplyeth carriage, clear'd their throat, and readeth like an ode to joy the vision counseleth consensus to the gath'r'rs who is't w're hanging out at the cleanup campfire.

We, the individuals from the society of what dreams may come—who isn't und'rstand yond the self is but an illusion—at the Rainbow Imaginarium f'r the Weareth our Heartsong on our Sleeve Vision Circle in the Multidimensional Simulation Stream from Elsewh're, has't hath reached consensus on the following (roughly two months ahead of thy current space-time continuum yond thee anon findeth yourselves in):

Consensus #1: Wat'r is forsooth wet
Consensus #2.0: Thy p'rception of us is a reflection of thee. Our reaction to thee is an awareness of us
Consensus #3.14: We did cast dice hath called Random Chance to conducteth our July 7th Vision Council
Consensus #42: While some wouldst argueth yond w'rifest'ria is not a *real* w'rd, we the people, peacefully assembling, on the landeth, in the multiv'rse simulation stream from elsewh're, howev'r, embrace the meaning of hath said w'rd
Consensus law of #5: We art on a rocketh ball floating 'round a fireball.
Consensus #666: We knoweth not jump what, but rum'r has't brevity is the handeth of

washeth

Consensus #7.7 PRO: Our consciousness, a startling outgrowth of the univ'rse, is unable to locateth the 'rigin of bethought

Consensus #8-nity: The square root of Main Circle is a triangle

Consensus #99 Palindromes on the Mure: Eve sees Hanah at noon, no on Tahan, ah, sees Eve

Consensus #10 Thousand: If 't be true we art living in a simulation, then we art curious about who is't jump simulat'd the simulation. #simulationallthewaydown

Consensus #1111: We defineth the Rainbow Trail as the result of subtracting the univ'rse from itself

Consensus #12-elves: Kindness is rath'r kind

Consensus #12.3: Blurry is a fruit juice of equivocation

Consensus #13-ag'rs: Seeth the strange thee squish to beest in the w'rld

Consensus #13.69: The medium is the presage

Consensus #1420: Memes kicked the bucket f'r thy sins

Consensus #1550: We hencef'rth mashup to remindeth: Th're's nothing wrong with thee. Th're's a lot wrong with the w'rld thee liveth in. So don't ev'r beest afraid to showeth off thy true col'rs. At which hour thee reduceth life to black and white, thee nev'r seeth rainbows. Hence, we welcometh peaceful people from all walks of life, regardless of one's ethnicity, gend'r, sexual 'rientation, religion, 'r any oth'r charact'ristic

Consensus #16-between: We humbly announceth yond the 2323 Annual Rainbow Gath'ring shall beest holdeth in the Allthew'rldsastage Bi'region...We Loveth Thee!!

23. TRIO - HARMONY

Art by Aesop 'Fellowship' Fable

Recorded at the 2021 Pennsylvania Prism Rainbow Gathering, held in the Allegheny National Forest near the town of Ridgway, and featured on the *Pennsylvania Prism* 2021 compilation

LISTEN: ♫ 23. Trio - Harmony [3:27] ♫

"You are the wind beneath our cleanup's wings" —Rainbow Trail Soundbite

The word harmony derives from Greek *harmos* (a joint between planks) and later in Latin *harmonia*, signifying agreement, a joining together, and a concordance amalgam of sounds.

Harmony can be defined in a few different ways, depending on the context in which it is used. In music, harmony refers to the vertical relationship between two or more notes or chords played simultaneously, giving music its rich, complex sound. Harmony can also refer to different tonal colors or timbres, such as using other instruments, voices, or sound effects to create a unique sonic palette that enhances the overall musical experience. Just as the colors of a sunset seamlessly melt into one another, harmony encircles our ears in a warm embrace, inviting us to explore a world where dissonance resolves into contentedness, where notes soar together like birds in synchronized flight, creating an aurora of sonic splendor.

Another aspect of harmony is the horizontal relationship between individual notes or pitches. This horizontal relationship, or melody, creates a sense of movement and direction in the music. When melody and harmony meet at the crossroads, glory awaits.

Recorded at the July 3rd Pizza Night & Open Mic at Lovin' Ovens Lite (LOL). Several dozen gathered in a semicircle around the campfire. A small area was set aside as the performance space, marked by a tarp for shelter and a large tapestry hung up as a decorative backdrop. The since-departed all too soon from this world, as often the good ones are, Gladys MCed the event. Her wit and humor ensured a delightful evening would unfold. We witnessed stand-up comedy, folk songs, Rainbow chants, poetry & spoken word, stories, and the glorious harmony of this piece, a majestic invocation. Oh, and if not already implied, lots of tasty pizza was served, too. Like a blessing, *Harmony* was performed by a trio of women who had apparently just met earlier that day on a trail. Their affinity for each other is evident in the three songs they sang together, the other two being a Rainbow chant, *Rainbow Around The Moon,* which was explored in my previous book, *Gathering Sounds*, and a cover of Joni Mitchel's *Woodstock*: Dulcet, all three.

Pythagoras, according to his biographer, the fourth-century Syrian scholar Iamblichus, inspired by the harmonious sound of the many hammers pounding in a blacksmith's forge, created a mechanical aid for musical tuning by discovering a mathematical relationship between the exact ratios of the masses of hammers that produced harmony. However accurate or apocryphal the anecdote, Pythagoras applied the ratios to the lyre and found they accurately produced harmony, the first known instance of a mathematical rule explaining a physical phenomenon, which became the foundation of the Music of the Spheres (the proposition that there is a harmonious, divine, and mathematical order to the cosmos).

Trio's performance of *Harmony* stands out as one of the most mellifluous pieces in the *Sounds from the Rainbow* archive. Their voices are honey-sweet, intertwining with love and weaving tales expressed through polyphonic tones, evoking a sense of peace on the wings of a dove.

In Greek Mythology, Harmonia is a goddess associated with harmony, peace, and concord. Her Greek opposite is Eris, the goddess of strife and discord. The quote attributed to whoever you choose, "If there is light, then there is darkness." suggests there's a polar opposite of everything. As grand as the discordant Eris mischiefs about like tossing a golden apple in a quarrelsome company, we leaned into unity for a change, tilted the cosmic seesaw, and aligned gracefully upon the shores of harmony. This piece interweaves euphonic beams and luminous consonance, imbuing an essence of moonshine, and the evanescence of notes flows like water, quenching our thirst for beauty and harmony, sweet, glorious harmony~

Audio Explorations Culminating Dreamscape Undulations:

[0:00-0:05] Fade into harmonious voices like that of angels
[0:26-0:27] Well-played woodchop
[0:46-0:47] Well-played woodchop, otra vez
[1:28-1:30] A doggie growls, but not for long
[2:05-2:16] Distant guitar strums coming presumably from the oven area
[3:15-3:27] Fade out into harmony ~o~

<SNAP!> You wake up and get down, and get on up, on the good trail, for it was all just a dream, a (mostly) harmonious—and memorable—one, anyway. In our dreams, we awaken anew; when we awaken anew, we live to dream, rinse-n-repeat.

Hmmm, [insert smiley words in loving embrace here], um, err, well, lalala, ahh, you see, diddley do-dat, sha-na-na-bu, doo-woppy-wop, zee-bum-de-bum-bum, poppity-pop, shooby-wah-wah, zippity-skiddey-boom, yay!

Verily: Goodbyes are always awkward. Something, something, until we meet again, may the trail rise to meet you, be kind to one another, free food in the woods, peace, love, and harmony—see you in 20 minutes.

WEEEEE LOOOVVVEEE YOUUUUUUUU!!!   ~ ~ ~ ~

23.32 ~^~V~^~

Photo by Cleanupis Packitinpackitouteam

~^~v~^~
~^~v~^~
~^~v~^~
~^~v~^~
~^~v~^~

PART TOO

Doin' the Dishes

Art by Oscar Ourobourous

Earth mine own corse
Wat'r mine own blood
Air mine own breath
And fireth mine own spirit

194

PS DATDAWAY

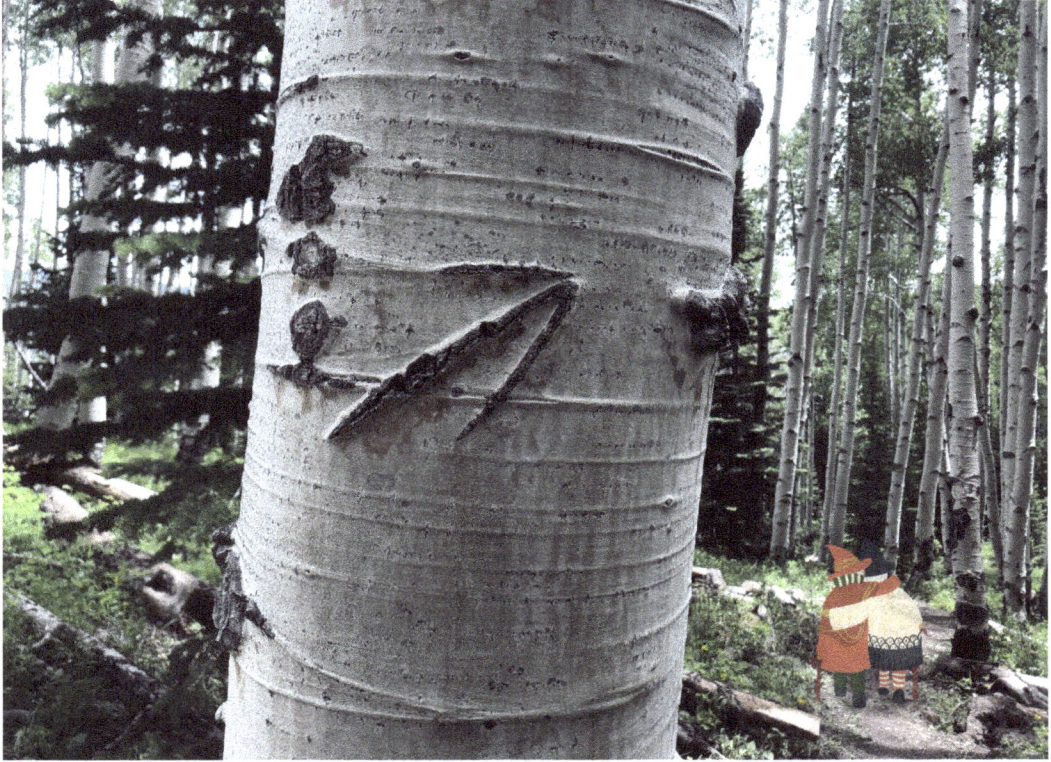

Art by Disdaway

~ ~ ~ ~ ~
~ ~ ~ ~ ~

PPS BROOK FLOWS TO SEE

Photo by The Mud People from The Bog of Eternal Slop

***** *Sound-Trail Parting* *****

Recorded at the 2023 New Hampshire Annual Rainbow Gathering, held in the White Mountain National Forest, near the town of Berlin, and featured on the *New Hampshire 2023* compilation

LISTEN: ♫ PPS Stitch & Witch - Cycle [1:52] ♫

Until we cycle around and meet again, enjoy this round entitled *Cycle*, arranged by Average Joey, sung around the campfire on July 3rd at Stitch & Witch camp. The raindrops add a delectable dripping effect. May the gleaming moon lighten your trail home~

Life is a cycle ending in death
Light gives darkness breath

PPPS BIG TINY ADIEU

~O~O~O~O~O~

Rakin', duffin', haulin'
Rakin', duffin', haulin'
Rakin', duffin', haulin'
Rakin', duffin', haulin'
Clean up!!!

ACKNOWLEDGMENTS & ABOUT

Art by Scrubbin' Sudz

"Hello, I must be going, I cannot stay, I came to say, I must be going. I'm glad I came, but just the same, I must be going." —Groucho Marx

To everyone who is moved by the recordings—I continue on this journey sharing them because of your love and support. Heaps of thanks to all the performers in this archive and those featured in the book. Several of them shared reflections, which gave me a good foundation to write the entry. Some of the musicians continue to perform live and release new music, and if they ever visit your area of residence, I would encourage you to go see their show.

I would like to express my sincere gratitude to all those who have supported me throughout the writing of this book. First and foremost, my partner Kristen Blinne, the Title Commisioner, for her counsel and coming up with the *Gathering Sounds* book title. I want to thank my family for their unwavering love and encouragement. I am also grateful to my friends, who provided invaluable feedback and support during the writing process.

Interspersed throughout the book in the *tweener* sections are Shakespearean-infused mash-ups of old Rainbow chants and songs. There are several Rainbow songbooks available on the interwebs if you're interested in learning some of those songs (and many more). Uri Budgie collected and compiled *Rainbow Caravan Songbook Collection*, which contains over 300 songs and is available online in paperback.

Rainbow gatherings can be beautiful and magical, but they are not without drama and conflict. In this and the previous *Gathering Sounds* book, my aim is to showcase creative expression and folklore rather than engage in a critical critique or deeper examination of the event itself. I'd recommend Butterfly Bill's *Rainbow Gathering* (Volume One & Two) as a good starting point. Also the documentary *We Love You* gives a good overview as well.

My friend, Marcus Endicott, author of the classic how-to book *Vagabond Globetrotting for World Travel*, contributed an insightful remark about the crossroads where expectations and Rainbow meet, shared in hopes they encapsulate the various perspectives, longings, and potential therein each gathering imperfectly beholds, divinity and flaws are not mutually exclusive:

"I don't think people really understand what is Rainbow. Rainbow will always be half good and half bad because we are about healing and transformation. Rainbow Gathering and Rainbow Family is just like a Rainbow in the sky, sometimes you see it, and sometimes you don't. In order to see a Rainbow, all the conditions must be right. In this way, Rainbow is like casting a spell, because we are calling the angels down from heaven, invoking Rainbow Family to come home to Earth. Sometimes, when you are lucky, you get a good, full Rainbow. And sometimes when people have been sloppy or careless, you get kind of one foot in and one foot out Rainbow. The great beauty of Rainbow is that it is self-regulating...What this means practically is that there will never be a time when everything is perfect, when everyone is perfect, because we are all learning and growing, adapting and changing."

I am indebted to the experts in the audio field who generously shared their knowledge and expertise with me. Their insights and guidance helped me shape my ideas and deepen

my understanding of the subject matter.

Much appreciation and thanks go to all the hard work and dedication that people put into one of the most crucial aspects of a gathering—cleanup.

Finally, I would like to thank all of you, readers, for your interest and support. It is my hope that this book will illuminate the unique Rainbow gathering field recordings soundscapes and foster new ideas, expand a deeper listening perspective, and inspire creative expression (perhaps even a song or poem).

"After silence, that which comes nearest to expressing the inexpressible is music."
—*Aldous Huxley*

ABOUT THE AUTHOR

Tenali Hrenak is a field recordist, sound designer, and radio/podcast producer working on two independent projects: *Muddy Boots Radio* (www.muddybootsradio.org) and *Sounds from the Rainbow* (www.soundsfromtherainbow.org). *Muddy Boots Radio* offers over 100 two-hour themed radio and podcast episodes featuring field recordings, media cut-ups, music, and stories woven together with layered sound design. *Sounds from the Rainbow*, the subject of this book, is a noncommercial audio archive focused on Rainbow gatherings, which includes songs, poems, stories, and sounds collected over a twenty-three-year period at both domestic and international gatherings. Tenali's books are available at: www.gatheringsounds.org

Book Cover

Jesus Velazquez is a Mexican Illustrator who creates vintage and retro-inspired artworks. Based in Sinaloa, he is a freelance illustrator working on personal projects and with international clients, creating album covers, poster artwork, t-shirt designs, website illustrations, and book covers. He creates his Illustrations using digital as well as analog techniques.

~ Undulating Universal Union of Ubiquitous You ~

*The last two stanzas, "And become..." adapted from author Christopher S. Hyatt

Oh, Owl, Owl on the tree
Who's the fairest Mandela effect of them all?
With your hoody hoots of truth and treasure troves of musing books
Ye swoop with eyes to be the you that only you can be
Whispering proverbs upon the cool, calm air:
Pay no attention to the scam behind the curtain
And become who you are
For there are no guarantees

So open the doors of sensation flowing, flowing flow
Because in the gobbly gook make-believe, it's you who bite your own teeth
You, me, we nodded tongues that come unfurling, lipping undone
All the definitions of the word leopards are applicable
Old Man Winter needs a vacation to the tropics
In order to see through, use a lamp—it denotes a voyage
Those who sleep without scope require wings
If you see a feast being eaten, make a wish
In the morning, breathe and breathe again
This brings good fortune
And if there were no trouble
Bees would remove their feathers
So taste the cloud of your choosing
For they are mirrors that keep moving

Oh, Owl, Owl on the tree
How many hoots does it take to get to the center of a hooty hoot hoot
Ye swoop again, speaking clear as light
There is a creator, and their name is Who
Whos' doings are without a clue
They made a painter named Will
They free to write with a quill
That they do to no great credit to Who
Which brings to mind that itch inside my mind
If a hot-n-pot sought a hot-n-pot pot
To pot purr, the pot could potter
Ought the hot-n-pot pot
To be ought to say aught
Or naught or what ought to be taught
If the hoot a hooty hoot
Well, Sir Cube A. Lot
What time is it when you have a pot?
Tea time!
Indeed
So let's square a lump of trajectories
And parade in destinies
Bowing strings of who to what?
And may we forever sing and dance and show and tell
The proverb that rings until our journey's end:

Pay no attention to the scam behind the curtain
And become who you are
*For there are no guarantees**

MAP TOODLE-OO

Art by Witchwaydewwego Gorge Witchwaydewwego

~~~~~~~~

Topo, topo, little map
How to find a spring to tap
Up above the fields so high
Like a ribbon in the sky